TRUE TALES OF PRESCOTT

TRUE TALES OF
PRESCOTT

BRADLEY G. COURTNEY
AND DREW DESMOND

Published by The History Press
Charleston, SC
www.historypress.com

First published 2022

Manufactured in the United States

ISBN 9781467151870

Library of Congress Control Number: 2022943540

CONTENTS

ACKNOWLEDGEMENTS

I would first like to thank Susan Tone for her invaluable editing. I have learned so much from you. Now, let's see if the lessons stick in future projects.

Drew Desmond, what a pleasure it has been and is to work with you! If the people of the world got along as well as you and I do, what a better planet it would be. I cherish your friendship, and you inspire me to try to keep up!

My dear and brilliant friend Bryan Gillis, thank you for your help with the Bruce Springsteen chapter. Bruuuce!

Thank you, Kate Anderson (also known as Kuki Hargrave), for the wonderful image of Buckey O'Neill when he was a Rough Rider in San Antonio, Texas.

Thank you, Whiskey Row Social Club and Historical Society. We have started something grand.

Dennis and Derry McCormick, thank you for letting me set up an "office" at the Palace—the finest saloon in the West—from time to time, and for letting me look important with my computer and papers spread across "Brad's table" while munching on a Cactus Country fried chicken sandwich and sipping on a virgin margarita with orange juice and Red Bull. Indeed, thank you to the entire Palace staff for treating Wendi and me like family.

Most of all, thank you, Wendi "Bradley" Roudybush, the love of my new life. In more ways than one, you have saved my life. You have given me a home, a new and invigorating way of life, a family (albeit of the canine variety) and a reciprocal love that nourishes my heart every single moment of every day. I love you with all of me forever.

—Bradley G. Courtney

I would first like to thank my wife, Pam. Without her, I would not have a writing career.

My thanks also go to the Prescott Western Heritage Foundation (www.visitwhc.org), particularly Melissa Ruffner, for keeping a close eye on me and offering support—in that order! Melissa and I share a love for history and Hershey chocolate. Thank you for the photographs, Melissa!

I—and Bradley—must also mention how nice it has been to work with our editor for this project, Laurie Krill. If only my mother would have proofread my material with such encouragement!

And finally, Mr. Courtney, sir: Well, it looks like we got another one under our belts, and now, as we put the final touches on these acknowledgements, would you *please* unlock the door and let me out?

—Drew Desmond

1

ISAAC GOLDBERG AND TRUE TALES OF PRESCOTT'S FIRST SALOON

By Bradley G. Courtney

Whiskey Row of Prescott, Arizona, is one of the true landmarks of both the historic and present-day American West. A visit there today is a welcome brush with the past; walking its sidewalks feels like a step back in time. But it is more than that—it is what the West has become. It is where the West is going. The Whiskey Row of today is neither an anachronism nor a contradiction but a symbol of the struggle to fuse the present with the past.

Whiskey Row was a microcosm of the frontier West and a world unto itself. Nowadays, it is famous throughout the Southwest, but its history and the sundry of true and colorful Old West tales it has rendered demonstrate that it should be even more renowned. A general understanding of the Row's origins will help the reader more fully appreciate some of the following true tales.

In 1864, the founding fathers of Arizona trekked from the East and Midwest in search of a proper setting in which to establish a government in the recently declared Arizona Territory. These ten men—known in history as the Governor's Party—were handpicked by President Abraham Lincoln. They were led by John Goodwin, a Maine man who had been appointed territorial governor by Lincoln after his first appointee, John Gurley of Ohio, died before taking office.

Several members of the Governor's Party had read William Hickling Prescott's epic literary work *The History of the Conquest of Mexico*, which had

Whiskey Row, with roots that go back to 1864, has stood the test of time. *Norman Fisk.*

sparked their imaginations. These members not only wanted to set up a government but to find fortune for themselves in a land they surmised might have once been occupied by rich Aztecs. That expanse today is called the Central Highlands of Arizona, and it is an area that has proven itself to possess vast mineral sources.

After a brief sojourn fifteen miles north in Chino Valley, the party eventually reached a semi-level section situated amid the world's largest ponderosa pine forest, and the "promised land" emerged. Within this mainly unexplored area, there was little else but mountain wildlife, a few tribes of indigenous people, such as the Yavapai Apache, and a few transplanted daring souls (mostly those prospecting for gold and silver) who were already risking it all in the hopes of achieving a new, prosperous and more independent life. There also existed what seemed like an endless supply of natural source material for building a town—wood.

In this picturesque environment rose a hamlet that, from scratch, quickly became not only a town but the capital of Arizona Territory: Prescott, named after the aforementioned preeminent historian William Prescott. It would also become early Arizona's irrefutable historical heart and soul. And the heart and soul of Prescott would become known throughout the West as Whiskey Row. Indeed, Prescott would become the "salooniest" of saloon towns.

How far back can the history of Whiskey Row be taken? As far back as the birth of Prescott itself in 1864.

As the necessary buildings for an official town and capital began to go up—government buildings, grocery and mercantile stores, mining supply outlets and places where townspeople could purchase items required for not only everyday living but everyday living in a remote mountain wilderness—saloons also began to appear. Yes, the wilderness capital soon became complemented by a collection of wilderness taverns—much faster than even church buildings.

As amusing as this might sound, this was not unusual for that period. It has been said that the history of the West was written in saloons. While this is an overgeneralized stretch, it is true that saloons were the social hubs of the western frontier. They were places for companionship, business dealings and receiving information, and they provided opportunities for patrons to enjoy games of chance, drink—of course—and generally have a good time. And for the owner of a saloon, it could be a metaphorical gold mine.

The first Prescott saloons mentioned in print were those run by John Roundtree and John Dickson during the summer of 1864. Both businesses were unnamed, temporary, primitive and initially set up for the town's first major celebration on Prescott's inaugural Fourth of July. Both got the job done. The holiday was a momentous event, with most of the four hundred or so original "Prescottonians"—consisting mainly, if not totally, of men—in attendance.

A *Miner* (Prescott's first newspaper that ran until 1934, using variations of that name) report stated on July 6, 1864, that "saloons were crowded with customers, and we will not say how much whiskey was disposed of—it might surprise our temperate friends from Tucson and La Paz. Nobody was hurt, although the boys waxed very merry, and some of them very tipsy, and there was no little promiscuous firing of revolvers." Dickson even had Prescott's first billiards table shipped in.

Roundtree's saloon was especially crude. It was quickly constructed near South Montezuma Street, and its roof was a mere wagon sheet stretched over two pine poles. The bar itself was nothing more than a ten-gallon keg filled with what one pioneer thought might be whiskey—at least that is what those present decided to call it. Roundtree's saloon may have been the first to be located on Montezuma Street, where today's Whiskey Row is sited.

Yet, the most frequent story told regarding the saloon that birthed Whiskey Row has been one that involves an enterprising pioneer named Isaac Goldberg and his makeshift establishment, which, according to legend, was called the Quartz Rock. It is one of a handful of Whiskey Row legends that, after persistent retelling, has been perceived as true history. However, there is the legend and then there is the researched version of it—the true tale. Let's begin with the legend.

Like most legends, the Quartz Rock tale has an amusing flavor to it, as well as intriguing characters. It is an endearing and enduring piece of Prescott folklore that is a combination of certainly true, distinct events and characters.

The legend begins with Goldberg improvising a makeshift cantina, a shanty covering a crude, wooden board counter, two bottles of whiskey and a single tin cup, somewhere along the banks of Granite Creek, which runs through what became and still is downtown Prescott. Granite Creek is the central feature and key of this legend. Goldberg's saloon, it was said, was named Quartz Rock. This story also involves a nose-less, AWOL soldier who, depending on which version of the story is being told, was either Goldberg's assistant and barkeep or Goldberg himself.

Goldberg's immediate success was guaranteed, partly because miners sought escape, often via intoxication, from the toil of making a living in the surrounding mountains. He soon ran into problems, however, when inebriated patrons became disoriented from gazing at the trickling water of Granite Creek. Some, it was said, fell into the creek while trying to cross on an improvised bridge. Consequently, the proprietor moved his business one street east to Montezuma Street, putting a more suitable distance between his liquor business and the stream. The relocated cantina, it is theorized, was the seed that eventually sprouted a crop of saloons that would later be famously dubbed "Whisky Row" and later "Whiskey Row" after the latter spelling of that puissant beverage became the accepted form—so the legend goes.

Unlike many legends, which are replete with adornments and contortions of the truth, the Quartz Rock legend is merely a distortion that includes real people and combines two real but different businesses. Was Prescott's first saloon a makeshift shanty? It appears that's the most likely scenario, but it was not called the Quartz Rock. The Quartz Rock was indeed a real saloon, and its story is told in chapter 2. But the true Isaac Goldberg and the Quartz Rock stories are unrelated.

There was an Isaac Goldberg, and he told his story in 1894 to the Society of Arizona Pioneers. He related how he had arrived in the Prescott area during the early spring of 1864, just when a functional territorial government was being set up. Goldberg did set up a saloon of sorts with a "[wooden] counter, which concealed sundry bottles of whiskey," just as the legend says. And this plank bar did indeed expose only two bottles. Goldberg served his whiskey by the dram, poured into a tin cup and sold to one customer at a time.

Goldberg was not nose-less, but his assistant, or "bar-keeper," was a soldier whose nose, like the legend states, was mostly missing. This man had deserted an unspecified post, most likely from the Confederate army of the Civil War, which was still being fought when the saloon was operating while Prescott was being established. Nevertheless, Goldberg thought of him as "a brave man." Goldberg did not divulge the name of his bartender but said that he took good care of him. He provided him with shelter and paid him one hundred dollars per month.

How could Goldberg afford to pay such a salary? First, he charged fifty cents per dram, which would be worth almost nine dollars at the time of this writing. Couple that with the fact that one dram is roughly one-eighth of an ounce, a little more than a teaspoon—barely a splash. Today, a shot of whiskey is roughly eight to twelve drams. Indeed, a single bottle of whiskey was a hefty "gold nugget" that could be separated into individual drinks and turned into quite a profit producer. As previously mentioned, a saloon was a gold mine itself. Goldberg's business was also the most accessible saloon for miners and Fort Whipple soldiers—if not the only one of its kind before July 4, 1864.

Goldberg never mentioned a creek or the saloon even being near one, but a pencil-drawn map, dated 1864 and stored in the Sharlot Hall Museum Library and Archives of Prescott, shows a drawing of a structure with a caption above it: "Prescott's first saloon." On this crude map, it is seen on the east bank of Granite Creek at the junction of Carleton and Granite Streets. The map was most likely drawn by one of Prescott's first pioneers, George Barnard (who is described later in this chapter), while he was living out his last days in the Arizona Pioneer's Home in Prescott in 1911 or later. Barnard and Goldberg were friends and business partners for a short time between 1864 and 1865.

Goldberg shared a story that inferred his business was not exactly "downtown" (which isn't saying much because there was very little to Prescott at the time), or at the very least, it demonstrated just how vulnerable original Prescottonians were now that they, in essence, had become part of the wilderness that had no police protection. Enabling men to become inebriated in such an environment wasn't always a good idea.

One morning after a busy night, Goldberg found himself under the gun of "a rough customer" with "blood-shot eyes." The visitor's intentions were

In this earliest known image of Prescott (circa 1869), it can be seen that there was very little to the town during its early years. *Sharlot Hall Museum.*

clearly unfriendly. Goldberg, however, had a near-full cup of whiskey in his hand, which he used to his advantage by dashing its contents into the eyes of this landlocked pirate, temporarily blinding him. Goldberg and his assistant then overpowered the ruffian and threw him into their "chamber of penance," which Goldberg described as a frail "adjacent log-pen."

The prisoner soon escaped. Angered and still drunk, the amateur outlaw pined for vengeance and hunted for the whiskey sellers, but both had disappeared into the pines. Later, when the man sobered up and Goldberg returned to his liquor shop, the humbled hooligan sunk into remorse and came by to apologize for his "meanness."

Goldberg never disclosed a name for his business. Likely, it bore no appellation at all.

Goldberg did indeed move his business into the heart of the six-month-old town but not to Montezuma Street as the legend claims. He moved to the southeast corner of Cortez and Goodwin Streets. In doing so, he honchoed Prescott's first wholesale/retail liquor business. But some explanation is required.

In the thirteenth *Miner*, dated September 13, 1864, Goldberg advertised his enterprise for the first time, the first Prescott liquor wholesaler/retailer to do so. This advertisement pointed out that Goldberg had migrated from La Paz, a short-lived southwestern Arizona Territory town situated next to the Colorado River. Goldberg, the advertisement noted, was now selling his wares out of George Barnard's Juniper House.

The Juniper House was founded by the previously mentioned George Barnard, a multifaceted pioneer who, like Goldberg, had journeyed up from La Paz. Barnard, a native Michigander, was one of several original Prescottonians who had initially made his way west after hearing about the discovery of gold on Sutter's Creek in California. Like several other 1849 argonauts, he later moved to Arizona after learning of mineral strikes there. Some historians have pointed out that many of those Arizona pioneers who came from California after the gold rush never knew what gold looked like until they made an about-face and prospected in Arizona.

The Juniper House serves as an exemplar of how the first service-oriented businesses were built using the resources readily available in the area.

Prescott was still basically an idea, if not a dream, in the summer of 1864. Less than a year prior, there was a semi-village anxiously hurrying to not only be a real town but the political and commercial center of the Arizona Territory. When Prescott's first Fourth of July rolled around, with the Civil War still raging and the future of the United States hanging in the balance, it was critical for those first Prescottonians, who were overwhelmingly pro-Union, to celebrate the holiday properly. For entrepreneurs, it was time to get a provisional business in place to open on the Fourth of July and think of the long term later.

Named "by the boys" because of the sizable juniper tree by which Barnard conducted his business, the Juniper House was undeniably Prescott's first go-to food and beverage spot. It, too, began in the most pioneer of ways. One witness noted that the "progressively inclined" Barnard had "no house nor stove" when he successfully opened for business on the first Independence Day in Prescott. Rather, he cooked his cuisine over an open campfire by that juniper tree. Customers found it convenient that after their repasts were dished out, they could move to the shady side of the tree to more comfortably enjoy them.

Eventually, nail and lumber sheltered a workable restaurant where Goldberg's liquors provided a welcome addition.

When July 4 rolled around, Barnard was ready to go. He served breakfast, lunch and dinner; his bill of fare featured beef, mutton and venison recipes.

Barnard's menu was a hit, as the Juniper House was "largely patronized" that Independence Day.

There were more dishes offered than what was reported. From another noteworthy pioneer, Charles Genung, Barnard purchased sixty-two pounds of elderberries at a dollar per pound, and with them, he made numerous pies to sell at the event. These pastries were also used as a currency. Barnard had employed the Miller brothers, Jacob and Sam, to haul logs to the site where he planned to erect his restaurant, and he paid them in elderberry pies.

The pencil-drawn map referred to earlier that was probably drawn by Barnard himself and dated 1864 shows a cabin-like structure labeled "Juniper House," and it is located on the southeast corner of Cortez and Goodwin Streets, one block from the area sectioned off today on Montezuma Street and labeled Whiskey Row.

Although this map was most likely drawn from memory by the original Prescottonian many years later, the drawing representing the Juniper House does indeed fit the description of it from another influential pioneer named Albert Banta. Banta depicted the original restaurant portion of the Juniper House as being "a spacious dining hall." In reality, it was a twelve-by-fifteen-foot room constructed from a collection of pine poles. A single table made from halved logs placed side by side, flat sides up, was featured in the middle of the room. As sturdy as those split pine logs were, they presented a problem for prissier patrons: "The pitch oozed in gobs from

The Juniper House was Prescott's first restaurant. *Bradley G. Courtney.*

the split surface of the pine poles, and one had to have a care, lest his bread or other things got stuck in the pitch."

The food was "the best the country afforded." Fried venison was an oft-featured specialty. It might have been accompanied by stewed apples that were dried in the desert heat. Breakfast sometimes consisted of pancakes topped with a creatively homespun version of syrup that apparently made a rather humorous presentation. Barnard charged one dollar in gold for each meal, which was a hefty price at the time.

The Juniper House, however, slowly floundered and then met a sudden demise in 1865, after falling victim to the first of many destructive fires that plagued Prescott and Whiskey Row. Some believed the Juniper House was already on its way out financially because Barnard was too munificent and trusting toward his customers. Perhaps because he was not only the restaurant's chef but entire culinary department and service staff and did not have the time or means to check whether a patron paid. Therefore, he wound up preparing and serving too many meals for free.

Still flourishing in 1865, however, was Prescott's first go-to saloon, the Quartz Rock, the true tales of which are told in the next chapter.

2

THE REAL QUARTZ ROCK SALOON AND THE BARBARIANS

By Bradley G. Courtney

The Quartz Rock/Isaac Goldberg legend has had long-lasting and pervasive effects on former Whiskey Row history narratives, especially regarding the Row's origins. Even the famous Palace Restaurant and Saloon, the centerpiece of modern-day Whiskey Row and the oldest saloon in Arizona, has been incorrectly linked to Goldberg.

As revealed in this book's first chapter, the actual establishment from which Goldberg eventually hawked his wares was George Barnard's Juniper House, not the Quartz Rock. But there was a Quartz Rock Saloon, and it was crucial to the evolution of Whiskey Row.

The Quartz Rock was established by a man who never resided in Prescott. Ironically, in the same *Miner* in which Goldberg took out an advertisement announcing that his dram shop was now being run from the Juniper House, the venerable pioneer William Hardy announced he would soon be establishing businesses in Prescott. Hardy, a native New Yorker, was an energetic entrepreneur and a key figure in the nascent Arizona Territory. Probably foremost among his accomplishments was the founding the lower Colorado River town Hardyville, Arizona, which is now known as Bullhead City. Hardy also helped establish a toll road between Hardyville and Prescott.

The September 21, 1864, *Miner* reported that Hardy had "lately made a hurried visit to Prescott with a view of opening a business establishment here." Hardy recognized that with the founding of the territorial capital in

William Hardy, although he never lived in Prescott, founded the Quartz Rock Saloon. *Sharlot Hall Museum.*

the recently created Prescott, the town would soon be a center of considerable activity and commerce and would harbor the advantages of hosting the government. It did not hurt that Fort Whipple and its soldiers were also nearby and that the area would soon be teeming with even more miners.

Hardy actually had two enterprises planned. At first, the denizens of Prescott only knew that one establishment would be a store offering a much-needed "miscellaneous assortment of goods" on Granite Street. Within two months, townsfolk learned Hardy's second business would be located next to this store and would be a saloon.

Just as George Barnard had done prior to erecting the historic Juniper House, Hardy employed Jacob and Sam Miller to haul logs to the sites where his businesses would be built. The *Miner* was excited to report that "when such driving men as Jacob and Sam Miller and Mr. Hardy unite, there is business ahead."

When the saloon's grand opening neared, Hardy and his associates enticed customers by publicizing that on-the-house samples of higher-quality libations would be offered. On November 14, 1864, Hardy, with great ceremony, opened his bar.

Attending this inauguration was an extemporarily established local club of elite townsmen. With tongues plainly planted in the corners of their respective mouths, they called themselves the Barbarians, perhaps because they were living in a wilderness they never dreamed they would be in. Their mission was to "properly [celebrate] important events" that marked Prescott's progress. The Barbarians were led by Judge William Berry, and their members included Governor John Goodwin, Secretary Richard McCormick and several officers from Fort Whipple.

On the night of the bar's opening, the Barbarians' celebration was threefold. Opening a bar featuring the best billiard table in the territory and offering "a better class of liquors than we have been used to in Prescott" was certainly, in their minds, significant progress. There was also the momentous completion of the territory's first legislative session, which had concluded four days prior, to commemorate. There was another noteworthy event for the Barbarians to memorialize. In what was possibly the first marriage in Prescott, Arizona's first speaker of the house, William

Above: Richard McCormick, the Arizona Territory's first secretary, was a member of the Barbarians. *Sharlot Hall Museum.*

Opposite: William Claude Jones was the Arizona Territory's first speaker of the house. *Bradley G. Courtney.*

Claude Jones, married Caroline Stephens, who had arrived with her family in Prescott from Texas on October 5.

A shivaree was in order. The whirlwind wedding between Jones and Stephens took place on November 13, the night before the Quartz Rock opened. When members of the new territorial government learned of

Jones's marriage, they were shocked and seemingly amused that Jones's bride was only fifteen years old, some forty years his junior. Jones became the butt of some frontier jocosity and the Barbarians' first victim.

Jones was quite knowledgeable about the supposed history of the new territory regarding the Aztec Empire. It was believed that their empire extended as far as the Central Arizona Highlands, although that was not the case. Earlier, because of a great interest in the Aztecs among Jones's colleagues, he had been asked to give a series of public lectures on the subject, which he did. This would come back to haunt him. They poked fun at Jones by attesting that he, like the Aztec men he admired, had courted "a young virgin." The Barbarians quipped in the *Miner* that Jones had been "permitted to roam about of nights and make the acquaintance of parents who had marriageable daughters" like the Aztecs of old.

Before the Barbarians made their way to the newlyweds' house on the night of November 14, they grabbed all the "inharmonious instruments" they could carry. Judge Berry led the mock serenade with "a huge piece of sheet iron, upon which he beat most lustily with a crooked club." Secretary McCormick "whipped a bar of steel." Most hilariously, Governor John Goodwin hid in a thicket while beating incessantly on a tin pan, as if frontier paparazzi was lurking nearby.

Neither the bride nor groom surfaced right away, so the Barbarians forced their way into the house and "shook hands with the groom and kissed the bride." As might be expected, the teenage bride was sobbing uncontrollably and "panting with fright," which caused the Barbarians to depart and march straight over to Hardy's saloon to celebrate its opening.

Mr. and Mrs. Jones bolted to Tucson within the next few days and did not return to Prescott until April 1865. Jones disappeared from Prescott on May 5, abandoning his young wife, and never returned.

The grand opening of Hardy's saloon was considered Prescott's first soirée. The local population was heavily lopsided with males in 1864, but on this occasion, almost a dozen ladies were present, and the gentlemen danced the night away with them.

For three more weeks, the first Granite Street bar was simply called "Hardy's new billiard room" or "saloon" by locals. It "attract[ed] much attention," something that had never been said before about the other saloons in town at that time. On December 14, 1864, the public would learn its name: the Quartz Rock. Although Hardy owned this property, he did not have much to do with the running of the bar, as he spent most of his days in Hardyville.

An Irishman, John "J.P." Bourke, originally ran the Quartz Rock. Bourke was one reason the Quartz Rock immediately became a "popular resort." This was only the beginning for this Irishman, as he later established the Prescott Hotel. He later moved into law enforcement, serving two terms as sheriff of Yavapai County, and this was followed by his election to the post of county recorder. Interestingly, he was also the stepfather-in-law of Johnny Behan of Tombstone infamy. Unfortunately, Bourke, whose intellect was said to be "of the highest order," was gone too soon. He died at the age of forty-one on March 6, 1868. His memorial service took place on a miserably rainy day, yet nearly every citizen of Prescott attended.

Both of Bourke's bartenders became prominent influences in Whiskey Row's history. One was Andrew Moeller, nicknamed "Doc." Why he was called "Dr. Moeller" is a mystery, as there is no evidence he ever practiced medicine. Moeller would become not only a major Whiskey Row figure but one of the all-time great property magnates of Prescott. The other bartender was Joe Crane. The "jovial" Crane would follow Moeller in another innovative saloon venture, the Diana Saloon, and become one of early Whiskey Row's most beloved barkeepers and proprietors. The first Quartz Rock newspaper advertisements lured patrons in by telling them that if they wanted proof that the Quartz Rock furnished the finest liquors, they should "call and see DOC & JOE."

Andrew "Doc" Moeller started as a bartender at the Quartz Rock but eventually owned the saloon. *Sharlot Hall Museum.*

As is divulged in chapter 1, the Quartz Rock's legend is a mixture of true events and characters from Prescott history. So, what about the part of the legend that is consistently repeated—that after many had become dizzy or nauseous from the sight of Granite Creek's running water or had fallen into the creek after a few too many drinks, the Quartz Rock itself was moved to Montezuma Street and thus became the first Whiskey Row saloon?

This part of the story most likely stems from a transformation over time—perhaps from mishearing—of a statement that was attributed to a Prescott old-timer and printed in a 1938 *Arizona Highways* article: "'The sight of water made the customers sick,' so they built the *rest of 'em* [italics added] up on Montezuma Street and called it Whiskey Row." The saloon's proximity to Granite Creek may have indeed been the liquor dealer's conundrum, and the solution was found one street over. Most of the saloons were indeed built one street over on Montezuma Street—but not the Quartz Rock.

For almost four years, the Quartz Rock was Prescott's leading tavern. Even if there were drunken men falling into Granite Creek or feeling unwell because of it, the Quartz Rock lived on and remained in one place, operating successfully on Granite Street for almost seven years. Did the Quartz Rock play a part in the birth and formation of Whiskey Row? It most certainly did. At the very least, it was the beginning of a block that has accommodated many saloons.

Being Prescott's first get-together hub, the Quartz Rock hosted several colorful frontier stories. One undated but early story occurred during the period when Prescott's primary concern was "Indian troubles." Lately, Native signals—pseudo coyote yips and owl hoots—had been echoing back and forth throughout the forested hills, buttes and mountains surrounding Fort Whipple and Prescott. The haunting sounds were thought to be coming from either Yavapai, Mohave or Tonto Apache. It was also observed that whenever scouting parties left Fort Whipple, smoke signals rose from mountain summits encircling Prescott. Yet numerous reconnaissance missions had failed to locate any of the Native lookout spots—that is, until late one night, when into the Quartz Rock walked a half-naked Sonoran boy claiming he had escaped from the Tonto Apache after five years of captivity. To Quartz Rock patrons, the boy described and pinpointed one lookout position. This information was relayed to the Fort Whipple commander. The next day, a unit of soldiers attacked the point, only to find, as usual, no one was there. Yet the coyote howls and owl hoots ceased. The Quartz Rock information paid off.

Unfortunately, what was probably Prescott's first saloon murder occurred in the Quartz Rock on June 13, 1867, around six o'clock that evening. A well-known pioneer named William Murray was playing cards with several friends when in walked a younger man named George Crafts, apparently

BILLIARDS.

THE "QUARTZ ROCK" SALOON
Situated on Granite street, having been enlarged and refitted. with the addition of a New Table.making

TWO NEW TABLES OF BEST PATTERN,

is now open to the public.

THE BAR will be furnished with the best of Liquors. For proof, call and see DOC & JOE.

The Quartz Rock was Prescott's first saloon to advertise on a regular basis. *Bradley G. Courtney.*

looking for trouble for its own sake. He "interfered" with the card game. Murray wasn't interested in suffering fools at that moment, so he threw his cards in Crafts's face. Crafts then pulled his pistol.

Murray was unarmed but somehow snatched a revolver from the belt of the man standing next to him. Murray fired but missed Crafts, who returned fire. Murray pulled his trigger a second time, but the barrel of the revolver ruptured and exploded. Two of the three shots from Crafts's gun hit Murray, both near his heart. He died instantly. Crafts was immediately arrested and incarcerated at Fort Whipple. He had come from a well-to-do family in San Bernardino, California, who would "be shocked at his connection with this tragedy."

Murray was buried in the Masonic Cemetery in Prescott. Curiously, the *Miner* reported that he left behind "an interesting wife." It is anyone's guess as to what the reporter meant by this.

Almost three months later, on September 9, 1867, William Hardy sold the Quartz Rock to his first bartender, Andrew Moeller, for $6,600. For four more years, Moeller owned the Quart Rock before it suddenly went out of business in a fire—the curse of Prescott.

In 1871, Prescott was so small size that Granite Street, only one street over from Montezuma Street, was considered west Prescott. There was no fire department at the time. The outcome of any emergency depended on the participation and efforts of nearby willing citizenry. Around two o'clock in the morning, flames were spotted coming out of the Quartz Rock. "Men dressed themselves hastily, started for the scene of the conflagration" and did what they could to quell the flames. Moeller, who had been living in the Quartz Rock, had been fast asleep. He woke up surrounded by flames, quickly threw on some clothes and ran to safety out on Granite Street. More than twenty of his barrels of whiskey exploded, and this guaranteed the complete destruction of Prescott's first legendary saloon.

A larger catastrophe was flirted with when combustible items, including one hundred gallons of coal oil, ignited in the old store next door, also owned by Moeller. The fire then roared north to the Pioneer Stable, which housed $300 worth of hay and grain, adding more fuel to the fire. There was great concern that the fire would spread to the row of buildings on Montezuma and Gurley Streets.

Dr. George Kendall proved to be the man of the hour and led a group of men who had run toward the danger: "Kendall accomplished more than any five men on the ground. He was everywhere, working and directing others." Because of his and others' efforts, the fire was contained and was prevented from causing a domino effect throughout Prescott.

The Quartz Rock would not be rebuilt.

3

OUTSIDERS TRY TO REFORM EARLY PRESCOTT

By Bradley G. Courtney

The reader might deduce that the advent of their social hubs, saloons, were more important to Prescott's founders than the establishment of churches. The reader might be correct. This was disheartening to some, especially the ladies—the "respectable" ones, that is—who were excluded from saloon life. They could not help but notice that an inordinate majority of the problems transpiring in their hamlet had their roots in saloons. And the fact that a row of watering holes was mushrooming before their eyes with still no real church established in Prescott was troubling to some.

Indeed, the years 1869 and 1870 found much of Prescott undergoing a bit of introspection and self-evaluation: "There is no use disguising the fact that Prescott is fast becoming a disorderly town, and unless something be speedily done to check the desperados who occasionally visit us, we might as well cease talking about law," stated the *Miner* on October 22, 1870. Several of these "disorderly" stories of this period are published in The History Press's *Murder and Mayhem in Prescott*, cowritten by the authors of this book.

Earlier in 1870, it was noted by the *Miner* that "[I]ndulgence in gambling, drinking, and other vices has been nearly as hard upon our people and country. But we have gone off our trail and must now return." It was also pointed out that the young village had more saloons and gambling tables than even some of the larger towns in California. The soul of Prescott, in the minds of many, was being poisoned: "We know our people would be better off were there no saloons in the territory," the *Miner* continued.

Then there was the issue of a blinding absence of religion in Prescott, as preached by missionaries Caroline Cedarholm (also spelled "Cederholm") and Miss Garrison. Cedarholm commented, "While the nice, attractive town is crowded with saloons, it strikes the visitor's eyes that there is no church and not much Christian life and association." Visiting preachers tried to infiltrate Prescott's soul, putting forth the gospel of Jesus Christ, but they were quick to add anti-saloon and anti-whiskey sentiments.

A popular publication in the 1860s and 1870s was *Harper's New Monthly Magazine* out of New York City. It featured a widely read column called "Editor's Drawer," which imparted colorful nonfiction stories that sometimes featured creative dialogue and hyperbole. Three months after an alcohol-driven, deadly gunfight in the Diana Saloon on the southwest corner of Montezuma and Gurley Streets, a Sunday church service was held at 5:00 p.m. on October 2, 1870, on the Plaza, directly across from the saloons on Montezuma Street. An episode therein would have made good copy for the "Editor's Drawer"—no exaggerations or hyperbole needed. The incident typified the state of Prescott during those first years

Leading the service were Cedarholm and Garrison, both keen on reforming topers. A large crowd composed primarily of men gathered to listen to the ladies. A handful were soused and "not so heavenly in character." Yet they listened intently when Garrison sang songs and offered prayers and instruction and Cedarholm served up "a very earnest, sensible exhortation."

The fun began when the program was turned back over to Garrison. She preached against the evils of alcoholic admixtures and made the claim that "the Bible said that no drunkards could enter the kingdom of heaven." Two of the more drunk fellows thought "Miss G." was referring specifically to them. The first responded loud enough for everyone to hear: "Well, we don't want to, Hell is all we claim."

The undaunted Garrison went on to admonish those there to turn from the error of their ways and that "Jesus Christ says his blood cleanseth from all sin." The second muddle-minded man reacted with, "Eh? What? How? Did [he] say that? G—d d—n him, I'll make him take it back." This, of course, caused an uncomfortable stir among the crowd. One wise and benignant member of the audience suggested the two intoxicated interjectors return to the saloons, a suggestion to which they gladly agreed. The pair wobbled away, and the resolute Garrison "went on as though nothing had happened."

The ladies' fire and brimstone had little effect on Whiskey Row, although every now and then, a soaker would pledge "to never get drunk again." The proliferation of gambling and drinking along Whiskey Row continued, and the Row became notorious throughout the West.

Cedarholm fell out of favor with Prescottonians in 1871. She had traveled to San Francisco to beg the, in her mind, more civilized people there to provide funds for building a church in churchless Prescott. In doing so, she felt it necessary to "belittle the people of Prescott." Cedarholm spoke of the Prescottonians' whiskey and gambling vices and asserted they were incapable of raising a church on their own.

After returning to Prescott, Cedarholm asked to speak at a local gathering. She was rejected. Her characterization of Prescott to Californians was not appreciated. And although they were not approving of the way she presented it, Prescottonians did not disagree with the missionary—they knew their town was heading dangerously toward anarchy, if not possible extinction. Something had to be done.

Eventually, Cedarholm and Garrison gave up. The *Miner* informed the public that "after a long and earnest effort on the part of these ladies to raise Prescott away up toward heaven, they became disgusted at their ill success and our want of godliness as a people and hence departed for the sunny south in quest of more tractable disciples. May your portion be a grand success and a prolonged absence from Prescott, ladies."

The first church in Prescott did not come along until 1875, eleven years after the town's founding, and it hosted seven different denominations. Yet, by the 1890s, saloons were an accepted and integral part of Prescott's life and economy—and were even symbols of the town's prosperity. The temperance movement, however, was gaining strength throughout the country, and Prescott was not safe from it.

More than two decades after missionaries Cedarholm and Garrison attempted to scare men sober with the threat of hell, the Salvation Army sent an advanced guard—two young ladies, Maude Bigney and Clara Clemo—to Arizona's most notable saloon town. They had obtained the use of the opera house for services and were expected to attract large crowds, as both were "handsome ladies." This they did, but some attendees were there to oppose the soldiers' cause: "Complaints have been made of rude conduct on the part of some young men who attend the meetings."

Yet this attractive duo was more formidable than Whiskey Row regulars anticipated. They went to the jails and held street revivals right there on Montezuma Street. An especially memorable revival was held in front of the Palace Saloon on Montezuma Street, one of their targeted "hell holes of Prescott." After the service, the pair walked straight into the Palace and attempted to recruit soldiers for their cause. Most candidates therein were not willing to volunteer—"the army has not yet succeeded in enlisting many recruits," the *Miner* said. The ladies tried several strategies, even offering people free meals at their new headquarters on South Montezuma Street: "As but very few have accepted the invitation, the inference is there are few people in Prescott who are not able to obtain their [own] food."

Even Prescott's "church people" resisted joining. Eventually, the ladies were compelled to abandon their headquarters. In its place, a saloon would be built by Jerry Barton, a well-known former, if not reformed, "Cochise County Cowboy" who had ridden with the likes of Curly Bill Brocius and Johnny Ringo of Tombstone infamy. The irony was not lost on Prescottonians or Barton. Barton invited Bigney and Clemo to his saloon's opening. He told Prescottonians he would be "rendering an ode and firing a volley at 8 p.m. sharp" for the ladies. Bigney and Clemo, however, were no-shows.

Interestingly, today, the Salvation Army of Prescott operates in the general vicinity of where Barton's saloon once did business.

4

TRAVELING TO PRESCOTT BEFORE THE RAILROAD

By Drew Desmond

In 1913, William Meacham recanted the story of his journey from San Bernardino, California, to Prescott in November 1871 to the *Miner*. He was "bent on the pursuit of health, wealth and happiness—to grasp a goodly portion of Arizona gold dust, which [he] had been led to believe could be scooped readily for the pains." Meacham had high hopes, but he could not have foreseen going through truly hostile, lawless wilderness, where killings were common. He traveled without the soldier escort that had been promised. Describing himself as a "tenderfoot," Meacham's knuckles must have grown white as he tightly clutched his borrowed Colt revolver during the harrowing trip.

The journey started with a two-day ocean and rail trip from San Francisco to Los Angeles, "then a small metropolis by itself," Meacham related. Then there was a sixty-mile stage ride to San Bernardino—"a hot, dusty ride of ten hours." San Bernardino was where one caught the stage to Arizona. When Meacham reached San Bernardino on a Sunday, he was informed that the stage to Arizona departed only once a week—and it had left the day before. Meacham and his party would have to pay pricey room and board rates for six days while they cooled their heels waiting for the next stage.

"Finally, the eventful day arrived—Saturday, December 16, 1871," Meacham remarked. Each rider paid eighty dollars in gold (three months' pay back then) for first-class passage on Grant's stage, "the Pullman train of the day and date." But before the stage left, an agent for the company rushed up to the coach and asked Meacham if he had a weapon. When Meacham informed him that he did not, the agent gave him "a formidable Colt's six-shooter" to have on the trip. The agent admonished Meacham "not to let it out of [his] grasp after crossing the Colorado River." Natives "had been cutting up some serious capers in Arizona…hence the precaution."

Between San Bernardino and the Arizona border, there were many stagecoach stops. In his story, Meacham rates them all: two being "memorable" but most being "abominable," and all charged four to eight times more than the standard fare. "Passengers slept the best they could while in motion," he recalled. Still, the party was in good spirits and reasonably safe. They had yet to reach the Colorado River and the dangers that lay in the wilderness beyond.

That day started inauspiciously enough, until it came time to change coaches at the Arizona border. Meacham's "attention was drawn to a number of bullet holes" in the coach. He was told that this was the stagecoach that was recently involved in what later would be called the Wickenburg Massacre. For Meacham, the bullet holes "almost took the starch out of [his] desire to proceed further." However, the party was reassured that such an episode would probably not happen again, and "as a precaution, a soldier guard would escort the stage through the dangerous places clear through to Prescott." However, on the leg to Wickenburg, the scene of the most recent killings, there was no promised soldier escort. It must have been particularly unnerving when the driver told his passengers to get out and walk behind the stage "so that in the event of an attack, [they] would not all be shot at once."

Equally alarming was the chilling sight of one of the dead stagecoach horses whose last act had been to pull the bullet-ridden stagecoach that was now passing by. Meacham noted that it "gave silent evidence of the recent [massacre]."

With thirty more miles to go to reach the military post at Date Creek, there was still no escort. The passengers spent the time nervously, with everyone diligently keeping their eyes open. Fortunately, they passed without trouble.

When they reached Date Creek, it was earnestly hoped that a soldier guard would be secured for the last portion of the trip. But as the coach driver talked privately with the commanding officer, the passengers overheard the distressing news that "on account of a fire…he could spare no men to act as escorts on this trip." Desperately hoping for relief, the small traveling party was completely dismayed.

From Date Creek on, their anxiety was at a fever pitch as they took a route west of today's State Route 89 to Skull Valley, which had a fearful

A circa-1885 view of Prescott from the northwest. *Ruffner Archives.*

reputation back then. It was an area where several deadly skirmishes with Natives occurred, including a sizable encounter just seven years earlier.

The tension and angst rose until they finally reached Mr. Bower's Inn in Skull Valley. Bower assured the travelers that the final leg into Prescott would hold no further trouble, and he accompanied them "with his trusty combine strapped across the saddle horn." It must have been heartening and exciting as Thumb Butte came into view.

The entire trip, starting from San Francisco, took nearly a month.

There were no bands playing when the group finally arrived in Prescott on December 22, 1871—just a silent, light snow. But the small party of intrepid travelers certainly must have been overjoyed and relieved. In the end, the "three passengers found their friends and acquaintances to rest from the long, tiresome and expensive trip."

Meacham's two co-passengers were Mrs. A.D. Boren, who was visiting her daughter (the wife of a jeweler and the first mayor of Prescott, L.B. Jewell), and Colonel C.P. Head, "a capitalist looking for a business opening." Indeed, Head found one. He bought a mercantile store from the Henderson brothers and ran it for many years. His business interests also included a mill and a hotel, and he became a well-known figure in the Prescott business community.

5

PRESCOTT'S FIRST ORDINANCES

By Drew Desmond

It was May 12, 1873, when the Village of Prescott's Council met to pass its first two ordinances. The two simple and quaint laws offer an interesting insight into the everyday life of the early, small settlement. The first ordinance dealt with the job descriptions of the four primary city workers. The second dealt with criminal laws concerning "breaches of the peace."

Ordinance No. 1: The Duties of the Four Primary Village Employees

First was the village marshal. He was charged "to arrest and bring before the recorder all persons found violating any village ordinance or order and to hold such person in arrest," the *Miner* detailed. The marshal was also instructed that any prisoners in his charge "may be employed upon any public work under the charge of the marshal." When it came to funding his endeavors, things were kept simple. The marshal was "to receive from time to time such sums for the keeping of prisoners as the council may order." At that same meeting, the council passed corresponding "Order No. 1," which instructed the marshal to "appoint one or more deputies [and that] such deputies shall qualify before the recorder before entering upon the duties of the office."

Second was the town's recorder. Keeping the village records was hardly a full-time job back then, so he was also charged to serve as the judge at certain legal proceedings. He was to hear charges brought by the marshal within forty-eight hours of an arrest to determine if a case was worthy of going to trial. He was also responsible for keeping track of fines paid and time served. It was decreed that those found guilty who could not pay their fine could work it off in prison at the rate of one dollar a day.

The assessor, of course, was to provide an assessment of "all property of whatever nature and kind within the corporate limits of the village of Prescott," except federal, county and territory property. Interestingly, the assessment roll of the village was to be "made up in manner as required by the sheriff of the County of Yavapai," the *Miner* reported. It was also stated that "there shall not be more than one assessment in any one year."

Lastly, there was the fire commissioner. It was his duty "to examine all chimneys, flues, stove-pipes or other apparatus…in which fire is used in all buildings now standing or that may hereafter be erected." If defects were found, owners were expected to fix them within five days. If they did not, "such owner…upon conviction before the recorder [would] be fined…any sum not exceeding $100."

The two most important public safety positions were those of the marshal and the fire commissioner. A telling detail of just how small Prescott was in 1873 was the fact that in Order No. 1, "The marshal is hereby appointed fire commissioner." He was to receive forty dollars per month. But this would not be the only source of income for the marshal. He was also to "receive 5 percent of all taxes collected by him and shall be entitled to all other fees allowed by statute." So, in addition to the duties of the marshal and fire commissioner, he was also expected to collect the delinquent taxes.

Order No. 1 also set the wages for others. "The recorder, as clerk of the council, shall receive five dollars for attendance at each sitting of the council," it stated. For his court work, he was to receive the standard fees that were "allowed justices of the peace for similar services." He was also allowed to charge fifty cents for each copy requested, as well as fifty cents for his certification of that copy. The village treasurer's wages, in whole, consisted of a cut of "3 percent of all moneys paid into the treasury." The assessor was to get seven dollars a day for his service but was allowed no more than seventy dollars to complete the entire job. The fact that the entire assessment of the town was expected to take no more than ten days also speaks of Prescott's small size at that time.

Ordinance No. 2 Defined the First Crimes

All the crimes detailed in Ordinance No. 2 were described as "breaches of the peace" and were punishable by up to a one-hundred-dollar fine.

It was unlawful to "draw or exhibit in a rude or threatening manner… any knife, pistol, gun or other deadly weapon, except in necessary self-defense," the *Miner* reported. It was also deemed unlawful to discharge any firearm whatsoever within the inhabited limits of the village. An exemption was provided for law enforcement officers and cases of self-defense. This effectively banned hunting within the village limits. One could be arrested for being "found drunk upon the streets"; using "loud, boisterous language" or if they were found to "incite or urge any affray or riot."

Finally, one needed to keep strict control of their riding animal. It was unlawful to ride hazardously "through the plazas, streets, lanes or alleys." But that was not all. The council's lengthy list of where animals would not be allowed is entertaining. It was wrong to "willfully and maliciously ride or drive any horse, mule or other riding animal upon any porch, sidewalk or under any [home or business] awning." It was also specifically prohibited to ride one's animal "into any dwelling, store, saloon or other business house, thereby terrifying the occupants thereof and endangering life and property." Considering just how specific this section of the ordinance is, one wonders just how often this had previously happened.

Eventually, there would be hundreds more ordinances passed in Prescott. Yet the charm of these early ordinances elicits a smile and a longing for a time when things were much simpler and Prescott was much smaller.

6

FAMOUS HIGHWAYMAN "BRAZEN BILL" BRAZELTON MEETS WHISKEY ROW'S D.C. THORNE

By Bradley G. Courtney

Daniel Connor "D.C." Thorne may have been early Whiskey Row's most influential figure—and its most colorful. He was a not only a story unto himself, but stories swirled around him. Thorne founded the Cabinet Saloon in 1874, and it became the heartbeat of pre-1900 Whiskey Row. The Cabinet is today's famous Palace Restaurant and Saloon, often voted best saloon in the West by *True West Magazine* readers and the gem of Prescott's Whiskey Row.

On the morning of Thursday, September 27, 1877, at 6:00, a California-bound stagecoach left Prescott. D.C. Thorne was aboard. According to Thorne family history, he requested and was permitted to ride shotgun alongside the stagecoach driver. After all, there was no better seat for viewing the central Arizona countryside. An event involving Thorne—and later, the Cabinet—and an infamous highwayman known as "Brazen Bill" Brazelton would occur that day.

Brazen Bill is considered by some historians to be the most successful stage robber of his time, especially in Arizona. In an article titled "Hoodlum Graduate" from the August 30, 1878, issue of the *Citizen*, a Tucson weekly publication, it was reported that Brazelton was orphaned at a young age in San Francisco and that "he, with a few other boy hoodlums, lived seven years in an old boiler—until the aperature [*sic*] used as an entrance no longer would admit them."

Daniel Conner "D.C." Thorne (*right*) was perhaps early Whiskey Row's most influential and colorful figure. *Sharlot Hall Museum.*

Brazelton, described by a correspondent as "the most desperate-looking character you can imagine—armed to the teeth won't express it—he was armed to the eyelashes," personally bragged that he killed a man at the age of fifteen, had murdered an entire posse of seven detectives who were pursuing him in New Mexico and had successfully robbed nine stagecoaches (at least five of those robberies were documented). A legend claims he could shoot pistols not only equally well with either hand but simultaneously. Reports also claim he was an exceptional physical specimen: over six feet tall, athletic and possessing "superior strength." At one point, Bill actually had a day job in Tucson, hauling hay, grain, wood and whatever else needed hauling.

Inside the coach was Ed Peck, the founder of the renowned Peck Mine. Peck was accompanied by his wife, children and elderly mother and father. Riding with the Pecks was Gus Ellis.

The coach was transporting several mailbags; a Wells Fargo express box, within which was a package of gold dust and bars valued at $1,300; another containing small gold bars worth $470; and two large gold ingots worth $4,000—altogether around $150,000 in today's currency. Most of the gold belonged to Peck, who also had a large sum of money on his person.

The road to California passed through Wickenburg. In between Prescott and Wickenburg was the Antelope Station, which was also a mini boomtown due to recent nearby gold discoveries. Eight miles south was where passenger Thorne would find himself in a life-or-death situation. When the stagecoach dropped down from a mesa into a wash, there, waiting with a shotgun, was Brazelton.

Brazen Bill often masked his face with white or black kerchiefs. He ordered the driver to get down and hold the horses by the bits; then he called for Thorne to throw down the express box. Training his shotgun on Thorne, Brazen Bill's next command was for the saloon man to step slowly off the coach. Brazelton threw Thorne an ax to smash open the box. After Thorne handed its contents to the highwayman, Brazen Bill then ordered Ellis, who was still inside the stagecoach with the Pecks, to throw out the mailbags. They, too, were cut open by Thorne, and their contents were given to Brazelton.

The winds were gusting that day. One kicked up at just the right—or wrong—time. According to Thorne, this blast of air dislodged Brazen Bill's mask, just enough for Thorne to get a look at the thief before he quickly slipped the kerchief back in place. Thorne had seen the criminal's face, which suddenly made him disposable, and Bill said as much.

Before carrying out this threat, Bill inexplicably asked the driver if the horses would "stand fire" at the crack of his gun. The driver said he thought they would but mentioned that women and children were inside the coach. This apparently was the reason Bill spared Thorne's life. The highwayman then jumped on his horse and fled with the loot. Inexplicably, he left Ed Peck's gold ingots behind, and Peck was never searched for the money he was holding.

Thorne, although questioned, never provided a description of the robber to authorities, even after encountering Brazen Bill again shortly after the robbery. One day in late 1877, Thorne was standing at the end of his bar and facing the Cabinet's swinging doors when in walked none other than Brazen Bill. The two had a quick stare-down. Both recognized each other. Bill quickly left the saloon, and they never saw each other again.

Thorne, true to his nature, was disappointed that the highwayman did not stay longer. The story he shared with his family was that he was so grateful to Brazen Bill for sparing his life and, in his words, "didn't even rob me; I would have showed him the time of his life, and the drinks would have been on the house." Such was the fleeting and only known connection Brazen Bill had with Whiskey Row.

Or was it?

Brazelton's criminal career did not last much longer after the Cabinet episode. After a stage holdup outside of Tucson in August 1878, one of Brazen Bill's confederates decided to turn on him. Bill should have stuck with robbing stagecoaches. Later that month, during an attempt to burgle a bank, this presumed partner let Bill's horse go, forcing Bill to flee on foot. Sheriff Charles Shibell formed a posse and tracked the highwayman down three miles south of Tucson. There, he was shot down. Afterward, his dead body was propped up, and two photographs of it were taken, one unmasked and the other masked. The *Citizen* noted, "Those who saw him after he was killed say he looked dangerous even in death."

After Brazen Bill's death, a bizarre report surfaced. Apparently, Bill had spent some time in Prescott before his stagecoach heist in September 1877. More than one newspaper claimed that Brazen Bill, perhaps even two years before he was killed, pulled one over on the people of Prescott in its Courthouse Plaza in the middle of town.

It was said that Bill rode into town, stepped onto the courthouse steps and advertised that he, of all things, would personally swallow a wagon wheel. But first, he needed to collect money from the would-be viewers, which he did. He then excused himself by saying he would fetch his troupe, the members of which "were making their toilet."

And that is how Prescottonians remembered Brazen Bill—as the "man who didn't swallow the wagon wheel."

The Cabinet Saloon's history, however, had just begun. Of all the pre–Great Fire saloons, it would become the most storied—although not necessarily in written history. When Doc Holliday had his famous winning streak on Whiskey Row with his lover "Big Nose Kate" at his side in 1880, it most likely occurred in the Cabinet, the chief gambling hall in Prescott at that time. Before his friends Wyatt and Virgil Earp departed for Tombstone and everlasting fame, Doc, not wanting to slap Lady Luck in the face, remained in Prescott on Whiskey Row for an extra three months. Arizona's most famous saloon story, which is told in chapter 12, occurred in the Cabinet as well.

7

COCKFIGHTING COMES TO WHISKEY ROW

BY BRADLEY G. COURTNEY

By 1880, Prescott's reputation throughout Arizona was that it had become so law-and-order as to be almost dull. While this is a matter of pride for most, it nevertheless caused some slight embarrassment among those of a rowdier frontier spirit.

Two of these pioneers were D.C. Thorne, described in the previous chapter, and J.A. "Scotty" Scott, who had purchased Plaza Bit Saloon on Whiskey Row from Barney Smith (the future proprietor of the Palace Saloon who is described in more detail in chapter 21) and renamed it the Plaza Bar, Billiard Saloon and Ten Pin Alley (often simply called the Bowling Alley Saloon by locals). Their remedy? The world's oldest spectator sport: cockfighting.

Scott took the lead by announcing "that there really was to be a genuine cockfighting in staid and moral old Prescott." The first event opened near Scott's bowling alley at 8:00 p.m. on Wednesday, December 22, 1880. A throng of "sporting men" attended. Eight specially bred fighting roosters were brought in for four separate duels. The fourth battle was the marquee matchup. It featured "a red Irish game cock and a [D]ominique, the [D]ominique with heels and the game without." Having heels seemed to matter little, as the feisty Irish rooster pinned the Dominque against the wall for the win.

The event was a huge hit and left participants and spectators begging for an encore. More than $500 changed hands during the occasion.

THE PLAZA

Bar, Billiard Saloon

AND

TEN-PIN ALLEY,

(One door north of Wells Fargo & Co's.)

Choice Wines, Liquors and Cigars

Always on hand

B. H. SMITH, Prop.

Prescott July 7th, 1879.

Rally! Rally!

——TO THE——

GRAND OPENING

——OF——

The Cock Pit!

Friday Evening, Dec. 23,

Over the Cabinet Restaurant, to commence with a

General Maine of Game Cocks,

To be followed by Match Fights,

DOORS OPEN AT 7 O'CLOCK.

dec21-3t

Top: J.A. "Scotty" Scott owned the Bowling Saloon and helped introduce cockfighting in "staid and moral old Prescott." *Bradley G. Courtney.*

Bottom: Cockfighting was a sensation in Prescott in the early 1880s. *Bradley G. Courtney.*

The reprise took place on the evening of Friday, January 25, 1881. It topped the first contest in terms of attendance, money, excitement and blood. Two roosters were killed. And there was controversy. Thorne had entered his own Irish stag (a rooster under one year old) for the main fight. Betting was high, and a few men tried to rig the fight against Thorne's athlete. His rooster would have none of it. To the delight of most in the crowd, the Irish stag "knocked the life" out of its opponent.

Cockfighting went on hiatus for the rest of 1881, perhaps because Thorne was out of town for several months on a trip back east. He was back in September and making "things 'talk' at the Cabinet." Toward the end of December 1881, Thorne announced the creation of the "Cock Pit," stationed on the roof of the Cabinet Restaurant behind the saloon.

The inaugural night was scheduled for December 23 at seven o'clock. A fight between two gamecocks that had fought a year previously at Scotty Scott's January event, Daly and Murphy, made the featured matchup for a purse of one hundred dollars. The event, as expected, was well attended. The money waged and taken at the door was considerable, especially "for a town of this size." Even though gamecocks Daly and Murphy were pulled from the lineup, four fights took place that thrilled those present. The second battle, which lasted thirty minutes, was the highlight. It featured roosters Garfield and Grant. Grant upset the favorite by killing him.

The cockfights may have continued, but the December 23 games were the last to be reported.

8

PRESCOTT WAS OPIUM CENTRAL IN ARIZONA

BY DREW DESMOND

There is no doubt that like it did in many other Wild West towns, opium made its first appearance in Prescott with the influx of the Chinese population. "It is no coincidence that 1869, the year the Union-Pacific Railroad was completed, was the year that Chinese began to appear in [Prescott] in significant numbers," the *Courier* (Prescott's second historically primary newspaper, which was founded in 1882 and continues today, used variations of that name over time) observed.

Thus began a most uneasy relationship with a drug habit that would grow and endure for seven decades. Publicly, Prescott hated opium. But practically, little was done to stop it. Ultimately, Prescott would become the manufacturing hub of opium for the entire state of Arizona.

Opium use was perfectly legal at first, but its use was always kept underground and out of sight. However, by 1879, there was no hiding its popularity in Prescott any longer. The *Miner* wrote "The Chinese dens of Prescott carry on quite an extensive business in the way of opium smoking. There are several persons, not altogether Chinese in nationality, who pay for the privilege of inhaling the intoxicating fumes from opium pipes in the celestial dens of Prescott."

Indeed, complicating opium's hold on Prescott was the fact that many prominent, beloved and powerful citizens had fallen to its charms, with most being able to continue their normal lives. This was true all over the West. A Narconon article relates, "Accurate American history tells us that famous names of the period like Wild Bill Hickok and Kit Carson actually frequented opium dens more often than saloons. It was not uncommon for some [people] to spend several days and nights at a time in these dens in a constant dream state, eventually becoming physically addicted to the drug."

In 1907, the *Courier* offered the following: "[A]s a matter of justice, the Chinamen should have the same right to get drunk on opium as the white man has to get drunk on whiskey. The [problem] is that while the white man persists in invading the Chinese opium dream habit, the Chinaman does not take so vigorously to the street the drunk habit of the whites." Despite this, the City of Prescott outlawed opium in March 1880, due in part to the fact that it was originally and mostly a "Chinese habit." However, there was little appetite to enforce the law. Twenty-one months later, the paper complained: "Over a year ago, an ordinance was passed by the city council making it an offense to visit or keep an opium den within the city limits. Since that time, two or three dens have been kept running without the least regard for the law, and no arrests have yet been made, although they are visited daily by quite a number of persons." The outcry did produce a few arrests, but the crackdown lasted barely a year.

Six years went by before law enforcement again took notice. In that time, the opium habit in Prescott continued to grow. On March 3, 1889, six officers raided three opium dens at 2:00 a.m., "capturing thirteen smokers in addition to the proprietors of the places," the *Miner* reported. Only half of those arrested were Chinese. "Those who are in a position to know, state that…the 'hop-fiend' colony in Prescott consists of nearly seventy persons, forty of whom are Chinamen, fifteen white men, four white women and two colored women." The "hop-fiend colony," as it was called, consisted of the people who spent their lives doing little else but smoking opium. There were still many more businessmen, workers, miners, cowboys and housewives who maintained active, normal lives while consuming opium.

In January 1890, a mysterious fire occurred. At the scene, a box full of opium smoking paraphernalia was found, leading some to believe that the smoking vice was somehow to blame. A police officer related to the *Miner* "that the opium smoking habit was spreading to an alarming extent in Prescott, and many a one indulged in the dreamy luxury of 'hitting the pipe' who were little suspected of it. Recent efforts…to suppress the habit proved unavailing, owing to acquittals by juries." Later, another police officer said that he was responsible for the box of opium pipes, as he had confiscated them from smokers without arrest.

Two men "sleep it off" in front of the OK Store, circa 1910. *Ruffner Archives.*

Opium was popular in Prescott, and as time passed, Prescott became popular to many due to the availability of opium in the town. A huge raid in 1912 demonstrated just how popular it had become: "One of the most sensational opium raids that has ever taken place in the southwest was carried out successfully yesterday morning in Prescott at about 2 o'clock," the *Miner* disclosed, "and the largest amount of the crude article ever known to have been recovered in one joint is now in possession of the government." The place raided was a so-called Chinese laundry on South Granite Street, between Gurley and Goodwin streets, and it was raided by five officers. It was believed that the "laundry" sign was just a front for "nothing more than an established opium manufactory and from which the entire state was supplied with the genuine article. Six kits of smoking utilities were also taken, while the vessels that held the dope ranged from an oil can to daintily made little receptacles."

The *Miner* continued, "There remained no doubt of the guilt of the two [Chinese], as three of the largest cans were steaming on the stove with the brown destroyer, and in a few minutes more, the final process of canning in little tubes for shipment would have been perfected."

During the raid, a young white woman who was under the age of twenty and of "respectable parentage" was found to be "hitting the pipe to her heart's content." Instead of being arrested like the rest, she was held as a witness. "The amount of opium confiscated [was] valued at several hundreds of dollars and [was] estimated to be about fifteen gallons; enough…to supply thousands of inveterate consumers," the *Miner* explained. The fact that "thousands of consumers could get their doses for several hundreds of dollars" bears testimony to the inexpensiveness of the habit. In today's currency, a session at an opium den would cost about four dollars. Indeed, back then, a trip to the opium den was often less expensive than a trip to the saloon.

The only recorded death in Prescott caused by an overdose from opium smoking occurred in 1914, and it caused great consternation. The *Miner* cried:

> *Opium Victims Run Rampant in City*
> *So Finds Coroner's Jury in Inquest upon Body of Harry Smith; Overdose Fatal*
>
> *We further recommend that the officials of Yavapai County, Arizona, and the City of Prescott either stop the drugs from coming into Prescott, or the sale of them, or to have all such drug habitues leave the said city of Prescott, unless they have visible means of support and if such people come here to get rid of them at once.*

Despite the outrage, it is interesting to note how the jury qualified its demand by saying "unless they have visible means of support." Everyone knew that there were many opium smokers who were quite capable of living productive lives and were doing so. Also interesting was the jury's naiveté in believing that the opium was being brought into Prescott instead of being manufactured in town: "The jury had before it experts who testified that Prescott was invaded by a greater percentage of 'hop-heads' than any other community in the state," the *Miner* stated. This was largely due to Prescott being where the "dope" was being manufactured. "The investigation went even further…[noting] some interesting evidence disclosing Prescott's unfortunate claim to supremacy and undesired publicity in connection with opium," the newspaper concluded.

One of the last opium den raids in Prescott occurred in 1934. Five police officers descended on 136½ South Montezuma Street. Two were arrested and held, two women posted bond and two other young women were cited for vagrancy. Eventually, Prescott kicked its opium habit. Unfortunately, this was largely due to the disappearance of the Chinese population in the 1930s and the introduction of a new "miracle drug" from Germany called heroin.

9

BUFFALO SOLDIERS ARRIVE IN PRESCOTT

By Drew Desmond

When the *Miner* announced in March 1885 that "it has been definitely settled that the headquarters of the 10th Cavalry [of Buffalo Soldiers] will be on their arrival in this territory at Whipple, and that a company of the colored troops will also be stationed at that post," the citizenry was apprehensive. They had read about "the inevitable [poor] reputation given the 10th Cavalry by certain journals in southern New Mexico and Arizona."

However, the proud Tenth Cavalry would quickly allay such fears, and the people of Prescott would become completely impressed by them. "Since their arrival in Prescott," the paper later wrote, "the members of the 10th… are as well behaved and as soldierly looking a set of men that have ever been stationed at Whipple."

It was May 1, 1885, when "several of the officers of the 10th Cavalry… arrived at Whipple," and the entire regiment was expected in six weeks. Since Whipple would be the unit's headquarters, it would also accommodate the Buffalo Soldiers' band. Yet just before the entire Tenth Cavalry was due to arrive, word was received of "the departure of Geronimo and some seventy Chiricahua warriors of his noted band from the reservation at San Carlos," the *Miner* disclosed. They were "supposed to be headed for old Mexico, and from Geronimo's record in the past, serious trouble is expected from the outbreak." Several troops from the Tenth Calvary were quickly routed to the scene before they laid eyes on Whipple or Prescott. As a result, it was

The Buffalo Soldiers' kitchen camp at Fern Spring, near Baker's Butte, circa 1886. *Archives.gov.*

only Troop B and the regimental band who marched into Whipple Barracks three weeks early on May 22. Colonel Benjamin Grierson, the commandant of the Tenth and now Whipple, arrived the day before. In early June, Troop D also arrived at Whipple.

After hearing that the band had arrived, Martin Maier, an enterprising owner of a beer garden on Gurley Street, successfully booked them to play at his establishment the following evening. The band also provided "excellent skating music at the rink," according to the *Miner*. Indeed, before arriving in Prescott, they spent a short time in Phoenix, where they "gave the citizens of that town the benefit of a serenade, which was highly praised by the papers of that burg."

The band became widely popular, and the citizenry expected them to be playing somewhere in town every night. However, this would come to an end when, after performing on the Plaza, the wagon that was carrying them back to the post lost a wheel. Several band members were injured, one severely.

After several weeks, the band was back in action. On the day of the funeral obsequies for President Ulysses Grant, the town's observance was delayed so the band could finish its program at Whipple first.

As fond as Prescott was of the band, it was even more impressed by the soldiers themselves. "Many ladies and gentlemen…visited Whipple for the purpose of witnessing the dress parade by the troops stationed there," the *Miner* reported. "The drilling of B Troop, 10th Cavalry, surpassed in snap and execution any exhibition of tactics ever given at the post by any body of troops."

Like any other regiment, the Buffalo Soldiers had a few personnel problems. One soldier who had a bit too much liquor unwittingly sliced open his own artery while "showing some of his comrades how he was going to carve up an enemy," the *Miner* reported. Unfortunately, the wound was so severe that doctors were unable to keep the man alive. Another soldier named Eugene Volcame sent money for his girlfriend to meet him in Prescott. However, when she arrived, "She formed the acquaintance of another member of the regiment who possessed greater charms for her than 'Gene.'" Volcame was so distraught that he tried to take his own life by shooting himself in the head with a carbine. However, he must have tilted his head back just before pulling the trigger, because he succeeded only in losing his nose.

Throughout the Buffalo Soldiers' entire stay, the only quibble that Prescott could cite came from the saloon keepers: "The 10th Cavalry spend less money for ardent spirits than any other troops ever stationed at Whipple," they complained.

The Tenth Cavalry's stay at Whipple would be brief—just under a year. These proud veteran fighting men were needed too badly in the field to let them sit in such a quiet zone as Prescott. By May 1886, they were gone, never to return.

10

WHISKEY ROW'S BUCKEY O'NEILL AND THE NEAR "GREAT FIRE" OF 1889

By Bradley G. Courtney

William "Buckey" O'Neill is perhaps Prescott's most famous and revered historical figure. He was also one of the most devoted patrons of Prescott's infamous Whiskey Row.

Buckey was a natural leader and a nervously energetic go-getter with an ambition that went beyond a run-of-the-mill quest for success. He also had a knack for stepping smack-dab into the middle of historic events. Beginning in 1882, after leaving Tombstone, where he worked for the *Tombstone Epitaph* (according to his biographer, Dale Walker) during the days when the Earps and Doc Holliday were in town, the well-educated O'Neill became one of Prescott's most active and influential citizens until he left in 1898 to fight in the Spanish-American War with Theodore Roosevelt's legendary Rough Riders.

Before the age of twenty, O'Neill had earned the sobriquet "Buckey" in the gambling halls of Phoenix. There, he became a legend playing his favorite game of chance, faro. Faro was wildly popular in the 1800s, partly because a player's odds of winning faro were higher than in other card games of chance. On the back of some faro cards was a drawing of a tiger, and sometimes, just the act of playing a faro game was called "bucking the tiger." Mostly, it meant a player was going for broke and betting it all. The latter meaning applied to the gutsy William O'Neill, who became "Buckey" because he loved taking risks

When Buckey first came to Prescott—where he lived for sixteen years—and discovered the Whiskey Row way of life, he continued to buck the tiger often, almost always with a Bull Durham–filled cigarette dangling from his mouth, lighting one after the other. At first, his card-playing moments were spent in the Cabinet, Diana or Sazerac Saloons; he later moved to the Palace Saloon after it became prominent along the Row. Buckey's audacious behavior surfaced repeatedly—so much so that his detractors saw his gambling as an addiction.

O'Neill worked first as a court reporter for the *Miner*. Soon, he established his own weekly, *Hoof and Horn*, which ran for about five years and focused on Yavapai County's cattle industry. In 1886, he was made captain of the local militia, the Prescott Grays. That same year, he ran for political office for the first time for the positions of probate judge and superintendent of schools, a combined office.

Since Buckey was a well-known Whiskey Row habitué, some adversaries were led to run a smear campaign against him. Buckey was portrayed as a reckless gambler and drunkard: "Though young in years, his bleared eye and flushed face give evidence that the nights of dissipation—the days of continuous drunks—are slowly but surely undermining a naturally strong and vigorous constitution," asserted a local newspaper.

Buckey, however, seemed to lead a charmed life. These attacks backfired; they made him more appealing to the common man. Buckey won the election.

Next came Buckey's two-year stint as the Yavapai County sheriff. And before he strode into immortality as a Rough Rider, O'Neill was elected mayor of Prescott in 1897.

Even if his Rough Rider experience had never occurred, Buckey would still be found in today's Arizona history books. Why? In the spring of 1889, four cowhands from the famous Hashknife outfit near the Little Colorado River in northern Arizona robbed a train near Diablo Canyon, about twelve miles northwest of Meteor Crater.

Sheriff O'Neill led a four-man posse that chased the outlaws relentlessly through the rugged areas of the Navajo Indian Reservation, as far north as Lee's Ferry on the Colorado River, through parts of Glen Canyon and southern Utah. Almost three weeks long, the pursuit proved to be an impressive chase and capture.

The apprehended men were taken to Salt Lake City and put on a train to Prescott. Along the way, one of the prisoners, J.J. Smith, escaped. Buckey went after him solo, but after six hours, he gave up and returned to the train. While Smith was still on the lam, the other three prisoners were tried, convicted and sentenced to twenty-five years in the Yuma Territorial Prison.

Eventually, Smith was recaptured in Texas and hauled to Prescott to stand trial. Buckey had to collect Smith's three partners in Yuma for his hearing, which he did by train. When they arrived in Prescott, the famous Canyon Diablo train robbery soon became a Whiskey Row story. It involved incidents that had never before been covered in other Buckey O'Neill literature.

Bill Crocker was a young boy when the convicts arrived in Prescott. A large crowd had gathered at the train depot on Sheldon Street to get a glimpse of the infamous trio. When it came time to take the prisoners to the county courthouse jail, they were posited in an open carriage. The feisty Crocker jumped on the back and rode right up to the courthouse steps, earning him a front-row view of the bad men.

During an interview he gave years later at Prescott's Hotel St. Michael, Crocker related, "One of the robbers, irritated by all the attention they were receiving, lashed out with his foot and gave me a kick in the pants and swearing at me to, 'Get the hell out of here.'"

Buckey had heard rumors that the robbers' friends were going to attempt to liberate the jailed men. During the evening of November 19, 1889, he placed extra guards around the jail and sent extra watchmen to patrol Whiskey Row.

The way this jailbreak was attempted would come as a surprise.

Around six o'clock that evening, the first alarm sounded. A fire had been spotted behind the Palace Saloon, which was then being run by the previously described Daniel Conner "D.C." Thorne. After the incipient flames were suffocated, the first red flag was discovered. Beneath the saloon's floor were areas saturated with coal oil. Some on the scene surmised it had come from an exploded lamp. Chief of Police James Dodson's suspicion of foul play, however, was aroused immediately.

Within forty-five minutes of the first fire and only one door north, a second fire was spotted behind D. Levy's store. It, too, was quickly subdued.

Three hours later, around 10:15 p.m., another alarm rang out. Sloan's Plaza Stable on Goodwin Street was ablaze. The flames were already shooting through the stable's roof. The opera house adjoined to it also caught fire and could not be saved, but the fire stopped there.

One report said that eighteen horses perished in Sloan's stable.

Some initially viewed the fires as freak occurrences that established a record for Prescott—three fires in four hours. Hence, it quickly became

a theory that they were set in the hopes of drawing Buckey and his guards away from the jail. O'Neill did not bite, and no escapes were made.

Bill Crocker stated, "They placed oil-soaked rags under many of the business houses *on* Whiskey Row. If Smith's friends had succeeded in setting all the fires, Prescott would have had its big fire (Prescott's Great Fire of July 14–15, 1900) [eleven years] sooner."

Smith was sentenced to thirty years in prison, but the incendiaries were never caught. Locals were especially angry because the horses had died in such a horrible way. O'Neill was charged with bringing the four criminals to the Yuma prison. He enlisted James Dodson to help him with the escort. Crocker noted, "Realizing the type of men with whom they had to travel, the train robbers created no disturbance and were delivered without disturbance."

After his two-year term as sheriff, Buckey endeavored in several fields, including white onyx mining in Mayer, Arizona, and the hotel business. Buckey and his wife, Pauline, bought a two-thirds interest in the Burke Hotel, which, today, is the beautiful Hotel St. Michael. In 1898, Buckey was elected mayor of Prescott. Within months, President William McKinley decided America should intervene in Cuba's struggle for independence from Spain. Buckey was the first to enlist in Theodore's Roosevelt's famous "Rough Riders" regiment.

Leading his men just before the Rough Riders made their famous charges up Kettle and San Juan Hills, a Spanish bullet—which Buckey had said he was immune to—struck him down. Colonel Roosevelt, with whom Buckey shared several notable personality traits and talents, wrote: "As he turned on his heel, a bullet struck him in the mouth and came out at the back of his head so that even before he fell, his wild and gallant soul had gone out into the darkness."

In the spring of 1899, Buckey O'Neill's body was recovered and brought by boat back to the United States. On May 1, he was buried with honors in the Arlington National Cemetery. To Prescottonians, however, Buckey remained one of their own.

In 1905, Solon Borglum, the brother of the Mount Rushmore National Memorial designer, was commissioned to create a bronze statue that would

Opposite: The venerable Chief of Police James Dodson realized something was awry when several fires broke out in Prescott on November 17, 1899. *Sharlot Hall Museum.*

Above: Buckey O'Neill training with the Rough Riders in San Antonio, Texas. *Kuki Hargrave Fine Art.*

commemorate Captain O'Neill and the Rough Riders who fought with him. On July 3, 1907, seven thousand people gathered around the cloaked monument after a mile-long parade that included some Rough Riders. Cheers erupted when Buckey's stepson, Maurice, yanked the ropes, releasing the shroud that unveiled one of Borglum's finest works: a straining stallion being reined by a cowboy-looking soldier, truly a giant Remingtonesque bronze masterpiece with a native granite base.

Today, when visitors ask who the man is on that restless horse, there is usually a Prescottonian nearby who, although they probably realize the statue represents all Rough Riders, will explain, "That's Buckey O'Neill, a Rough Rider who rode with Theodore Roosevelt and one of the greatest heroes of our town."

11

THE DAM, THE DRUNK AND THE DISASTER

By Drew Desmond

The Dam

"Besides being the largest piece of solid masonry in the United States," the *Arizona Gazette* stated, the Walnut Grove Dam "also drain[ed] the largest watershed in the world, being upwards of 400 miles of territory." But in the dark, early hours of February 22, 1890, heavy rains would cause the dam to "literally explode."

"The disastrous breach of Arizona's first major dam poured 4 billion gallons of water into a canyon above Wickenburg and killed approximately 100 to 150 people, although no one will really ever know how many people drowned," the *Courier* lamented. "The story of the dam began in 1881, when two brothers from New York, Wells and DeWitt Bates, bought a gold mine in southern Yavapai County and filed sixty-three claims for placer mining rights. They filed a claim for all of the Hassayampa River waters so they could build a reservoir dam and diversion dam for the mining operation."

The brothers found investors, and construction on the dam began in 1886. However, the two quickly learned that they could make more sure money selling stock in the company. Shortcuts and cost-cutting became a priority in the construction. "Wells Bates, the resident director and prime motivator, seemed to share the same attitude," the *Courier* wrote. "The fate of the dam was sealed when the company scrapped one spillway plan in favor of a cheaper one right next to the dam" that would prove to be entirely inadequate.

The dam was never a solid structure. An 1888 article in *Engineering News* described its construction: "A timber trestle was built on the longitudinal axis of the dam, and this was gradually raised as the work progressed, the timbers being left imbedded in the stone filling. The heart of the dam was wholly made of broken granite, as it was dumped from the cars [on the trestle]." When the loose granite reached the desired height and breadth, it was covered in masonry. On the upstream lake side of the dam, timbers, tar paper and two coats of paraffin paint were used to make the dam waterproof. In a cost-saving measure, the downstream side of the dam had no waterproofing, leaving it vulnerable if water topped the structure.

Unlike modern dams, Walnut Grove did not utilize a curved semicircle toward the headwaters; instead, it was built straight across. In actuality, modern curved designs are a horizontal application of the ancient technology of the Roman arch, long known for its ability to evenly distribute and carry great weights.

Even at the outset, the construction of the dam was criticized. The *Arizona Republic* wrote:

> *In fact, engineers of the Technical Society of the Pacific Coast had publicly criticized the dam as a structure "full of blunders mainly caused by company officers in New York." Other critics* [believed] *the concrete and lumber used was of inferior quality and that some of the work was done without supervision of the chief engineer. Furthermore, whatever abilities the mostly unskilled workers on the project possessed frequently were befuddled by too much time spent in saloons and gambling joints near the construction site.*

The worst economic decision involved the inadequate emergency spillway that was meant to keep floodwaters from topping the dam. "The dam leaked considerably as the water accumulated, as was to be expected," *Engineering News* explained, "but it gradually became tighter, and this leakage [was] reduced to a small amount."

"The reservoir filled up during a heavy rainfall on March 14–17, 1889," the *Courier* recalled. A minor enlargement of the spillway was ordered in December 1889, but the hydraulic engineer confirmed that the spillway was still too small.

Columnist Roscoe Wilson wrote:

> *Evidently, the placer operations along the Hassayampa below the dam did not come up to expectations with the result that in 1889 the company decided to acquire and irrigate desert land acreage twenty-two miles downstream. There, near the mouth of Fool's Gulch, a work camp was set up which employed nearly 100 persons appertaining to the construction of a dam to divert the river onto the desert to be used both for irrigation and gold extraction. This diversion dam was nearing completion when the great catastrophe occurred.*

Less than a year later, a combination of three days of heavy precipitation filled the reservoir to near the top of the dam and threatened its collapse.

"It was around 4 p.m. on that Friday when Superintendent Thomas H. Brown finally decided that he should warn residents downriver of impending danger," the *Republic* related, "for as many as two hundred lives would be at stake in the event the dam collapsed. A few settlers and a sizable number of miners were scattered along the river bottom below the canyon in a fifteen-mile stretch separating the big dam and the lesser barrier still under construction."

The Drunk

Brown ordered "one of his employees, Dan Burke, a prospector and miner who was supposed to be familiar with the country, to mount a horse and make the twenty-two-mile ride by trail to the Fool's Gulch camp to notify the people there that the main dam might soon wash out," Wilson wrote. In doing so, Brown made two mistakes. First, he hired Burke, a notorious drunk; second, he paid him in advance.

According to the *Miner*, Brown cautioned Burke. "'Now, Dan, you will not stop on the road.' To which Burke replied, 'No Mr. Brown, I will promise you. I will not.'" Burke then mounted his horse and started his mission by first going to a saloon to have a little nip to help against the cold. But one drink followed another, and soon, he was too inebriated to accomplish his task.

After the disaster, Burke wrote the newspaper to try to make amends and explain his actions. "The gist of his story was to the effect that after starting out, he had to swim his horse through two swift-running creeks," Wilson related, "which, with the rainstorm in progress, caused him to become thoroughly soaked by the time he reached what he call[ed] 'Goodwin Station,' which must have been somewhere on Oak or Cherry Creeks."

After wasting more time in the storm trying to find the correct trail, Burke said that he ended up back at Goodwin, where "he bought a bottle of whisky and then started to backtrack until he arrived at the Jim Cameron ranch," the *Miner* reported. It was there that a second messenger sent by Brown caught up with Burke. "Mr. Akard came along and offered Cameron twenty-five dollars to pilot him to the lower dam. Cameron could not go, as he had no horse." Burke claimed that he told Cameron to take his, since he "did not know the trail in the dark." Cameron rode off in the storm while Burke continued drinking and enjoying a prepared supper.

Not arriving until 7:30 the next morning, Cameron could only take stock of the destruction.

The Disaster

"Meanwhile, back at Walnut Grove, Superintendent Brown, lantern in hand, paced nervously but cautiously around the dam site," the *Republic* reported. "He was helpless to do anything, but he was the man responsible for giving the company a full report of whatever might occur. His lonely rain-soaked vigil lasted until 2 a.m." For six hours, he watched anxiously as water topped the four-hundred-foot length of the dam, eroding the unprotected side. "Workmen tried to widen the spillway in the midst of the driving rain, but it was too late," the *Courier* described. "The spillway was collapsing."

"At this point, the water was pouring over the dam in a solid body three feet deep," the *Miner* related.

> *When an immense steel cable, reaching from the tower to the bank...broke, with a loud report, and a ball of fire seemed to shoot from it. The midnight watchers were startled by it, and at first thought that a box of giant powder had exploded. The next instant, the tower was seen to totter and fall, when the entire structure, containing ninety thousand tons of rocks, seemed to move bodily down the stream, sweeping everything in its track.*

A one-hundred-foot-tall, mountain-born tsunami was embarking, and nothing on this Earth was going to stop it. Quickly, "the entire structure literally exploded into pieces with a roar that could be heard for miles. Down the canyon poured a towering wall of water, rocks, timbers and trees," the *Republic* recorded.

The boulders that made up the dam, ranging in size from heavy to humungous, now become the grit that would scour the canyon clean of every visible sign of life. One witness related that "when the final crash came, the roar of the waters sounded like that of Niagara Falls, only ten-fold greater, while the rumbling, grinding sound of the immense boulders forming the structure were indescribable. It caused a vibration of the earth."

"The one-hundred-foot-high wall of water, laden with boulders and debris, boiled down through the high-banked canyon below the dam site and began to spread out as the flood reached the…wider bottom lands. In little more than an hour after the dam burst, the two-mile-long lake impounded behind it was emptied," the *Republic* reported.

"In the canyon between the two dams there were quite a large number of cabins, all of which, with their unfortunate human occupants, were carried down to death and destruction by the rushing flood," the *Arizona Gazette* related. In about a half-hour, the wall of water had traveled the twenty-two miles to the lower dam. "It was swept away like chaff before a hurricane, and on went this demon of death."

By the time the wall of water had spread out and hit Wickenburg, it was still forty feet tall. Henry Wickenburg, as well as every other farmer in the area, lost everything. "Seymour, twelve miles from Wickenburg, was the next victim of the mad, rushing waters," the *Gazette* explained. "The store and ranch house of Mrs. Conger, with all their contents, were demolished, the lady escaping by fleeing in her nightclothes to the mountains."

The *Gazette* continued, "In fact, the entire distance between Seymour and the main dam [presented] a scene of indescribable desolation. The country [was] inhabited by Mexican herders and miners, and the loss of life sustained by those people will, in all human probability, never be known."

The tremendous energy of the rushing waters also produced a strange, unexplained, "earth-light" type phenomena: "One remarkable effect was the brilliant glow of phosphorescent light, which is said to have illuminated the progress of the flood as it advanced," the *Courier* related, "rendered specially noticeable by the blackness of the night." This light may have been caused by static electricity, sparks from the colliding boulders—or both. "As far as could be seen down the stream, not a vestige of a tree or shrub could be seen, the walls and bottom of the canyon being washed perfectly smooth. The only indications left to mark the place where the dam stood were a few strips of the skin of the dam and a very small piece of the west wall of the dam."

Survivor Accounts

While whiskey contributed greatly to the loss of life, it also happened to save several. According to the *Miner*, one dozen men "would have been drowned but for that which prohibitionists denounce—whisky." One of the men in the tent got up to get himself a drink when he heard the rush coming. He "alarmed the sleepers, who lost no time in climbing for places of safety."

One miner who never cut his hair was saved by that fact. The *Miner* related:

> *While taking his involuntary ride on the roof of his cabin, in the turbid and death-dealing waters of the flood, his cabin roof was thrown against the bluff by a mighty wave, among some bushes. His hair caught in the brush, holding him fast, when he loosened his hold on the rafters and grabbing the brush, was enabled to pull himself out of the water and climb up the steep cliff beyond its reach, where he remained until his rescue the next morning.*

Peeples Valley pioneer Ida Genung wrote the newspaper to tell the tale of how she survived. She attributed her survival to being awakened by a severe premonition of dread. Although she escaped in her nightclothes, her store and belongings were lost. The site was now buried under twenty feet of boulders, timber and sand.

"A young man named Boone showed great presence of mind by grasping his little sister and barely escaping with her from the jaws of the monster flood," the *Miner* wrote. A Chinese man arrived in Prescott after surviving the disaster. It was believed that he was "the only one of his race that escaped."

"Immediately following the washout of the Fool's Gulch camp," Wilson wrote, "horsemen rode along the banks of the Hassayampa for miles and found a good many bodies of drowned persons, the exact number not being given in any report....It was also thought that some of the bodies were carried clear to the Colorado River and perhaps into the Gulf of California." Dead fish were found eighty feet up the river's banks. Half of a man's face was also discovered.

"Upon the receipt of the news of this awful calamity in Phoenix," the *Arizona Gazette* explained, "relief corps were at once sent out, taking money, provisions and clothes to the suffering, and the county officers, with a spirit of generosity, raised $1,000 to be forwarded to the scene of death and desolation."

"Newly elected Yavapai County sheriff Buckey O'Neill also rode south to help, bringing along a doctor and several deputies. He found battered bodies for miles along the shoreline." The job O'Neill did was appreciated by all. "All the men speak in most enthusiastic terms of the untiring and self-sacrificing work being done by Sheriff O'Neill, who was in charge of the work of searching for and burying the dead," *Miner* reported, "They said he was here, there and everywhere, wading in water, floating coffins and shirking no duty."

The locating of bodies would continue for quite some time. One body wasn't found until nineteen months later, and, shockingly, another body was discovered by a miner thirty-three years after the fact.

"The disaster brought national media attention to this remote territory just one year after the Johnstown, Penn., flood that killed 2,200 people because of the same spillway problem," the *Courier* later reported. "It made the front page of the *New York Times*. 'This is the first of the great storage reservoirs projected in the territory, and it is believed that yesterday's disaster will operate to discourage the construction of similar dams,'" the *Times* wrote.

"So far as the force and effect of the water was concerned, it rivaled even the Johnston flood," the *Miner* echoed. "The only difference between the two was that this did not have a populous country below it to devastate, although it made a pretty clean sweep of everything in its track."

According to the *Courier*, "Major John Wesley Powell, then head of the U.S. Geological Survey, discussed the Walnut Canyon disaster during a congressional hearing. He urged future dam engineers to conduct hydrographic surveys and take the potential for torrential downpours into account."

The *Miner* pointed out in 1890:

> *The principal defects were: an inadequate wastewater way to carry off the surplus water in case of floods and an entire lack of protection to the dam in case of an overflow and deeming the precaution for such an emergency as unnecessary. Their work was, to a great extent, experimental. The defects found to exist in this enterprise are of such a nature as to be easily remedied in construction of such dams in the future.*

There was talk of rebuilding the dam, but it was never done. "Numerous lawsuits were filed against the dam owners, but nobody ever got a cent," the *Republic* recalled.

"Rightly or wrongly, the 'company' was blamed for the poor dam construction and for not acting more quickly to warn the lower camp of the threatened break. This resulted in a bitter feeling against it locally for a long time," Wilson explained.

"Today, about all that remains of the dam is a diversion tunnel, construction roads, chunks of the spillway and the heavy bolts which once held the steel cable that snapped when the dam broke," the *Courier* stated. "And more than likely, some of the lost souls remain buried under many feet of rock and sand."

As for "The Drunk"

Dan Burke was arrested by Sheriff O'Neill for manslaughter but was later released because the territory's manslaughter laws didn't really cover death by negligence of this sort. In an unknown newspaper article titled "Release of an Unpunished Scoundrel," (found in a Sharlot Hall Museum Archives folder) it was reported, "Immediately on being released from custody, Burke celebrated the event by drinking and carousing. Public indignation against him is very strong here."

Burke attempted to explain his actions in a letter to the *Courier*, but it completely backfired. In the letter, he claimed that some well-known and respected pioneers thought well of him. These pioneers included Henry Wickenburg, Charles Genung, John White and Stephen Condron. This immediately brought letters of denial and consternation from the four pioneers. Three denied they ever knew him, while Condron admitted he knew Burke for a long time, but "he never knew any good of him."

Nearly every other claim that Burke made in his defense was either refuted or denied. The *Miner* reported:

> *Mr. Akard, the second messenger sent…pronounces Burke's statements about swimming creeks as purest fiction and says that water enough… to have swam a horse would have swept Cameron's house away, where he found Burke so drunk he could scarcely walk across the floor. He also states that Burke absolutely refused them the use of his horse to continue the journey and that it was only through strategy that they succeeded in getting it. James Cameron confirms the statement of Mr. Akard in every particular….The law of this territory does not cover* [Burke's] *case. There are people here who say he should be hung, but as this is a law-*

> *abiding country, he will not be molested; nevertheless...life here will not, from now on, be pleasant for him.*

Burke got the message. He soon slipped out of the area to places unknown. He was long remembered but never missed.

The Walnut Grove Dam Disaster is still regarded by some as the worst natural disaster in Arizona's history. Yet this author would argue that it was all due to the folly and greed of man.

12

ARIZONA'S MOST FAMOUS SALOON STORY

The Legend of Chance Cobweb Hall and the True Tale of Violet "Baby Bell" Hicks

By Bradley G. Courtney

There is a touching legend that has been shared for decades along Whiskey Row that speaks of a baby who was won in a gambling game after being abandoned on the bar counter of a prominent Whiskey Row saloon. The tale has been featured in newspapers, magazines, books and collections of poetry. Of the hundreds extant, this is perhaps Arizona's best and most famous saloon story.

According to the popularly told legend—a mostly magical, "happily ever after" tale—the baby's name was Chance Cobweb Hall (or C.C. Hall). However, research reveals there was no such person—at least one who went by that name in Prescott. But a "baby left on a bar counter" episode did indeed occur on Whiskey Row, and it served as the basis for the Chance Cobweb Hall saga. The baby's real name was Violet Bell. She was adopted as Violet Hicks and died as Violet Binner.

Although the true tale has its enchanting moments, it is certainly not as glorious as the Chance Cobweb Hall legend.

There are many discrepancies between the two versions of the story. The Chance Cobweb Hall legend dates to 1927, when one of the most respected figures in Arizona history, Edmund Wells, published his frontier days memoir, *Argonaut Tales: Stories of the Gold Seekers and the Early Indian Scouts*. The work has been characterized as "a colorful *first-hand* [italics added] portrayal of early

The much-respected Edmund Wells created the legend of Chance Cobweb Hall based on the true story of Violet "Baby Bell" Hicks. *Sharlot Hall Museum.*

days in Arizona Territory." Within it is a three-chaptered section titled "Chance Cobweb Hall." Therein, Wells recounts in prosaic detail, twenty-nine years after the actual event, the story of a baby girl who was dropped off and abandoned on a Whiskey Row saloon counter. It concludes happily with who the girl became as an adult and her high standing in society. Over time, through persistent retelling, this story has become "history."

Why was the Chance Cobweb Hall story accepted as historical verity for more than seventy years? An original Prescottonian, Wells boasted a résumé of beyond-the-norm accomplishments that was several pages long. It is a record that includes him being the first Republican candidate for governor after Arizona was awarded statehood, a longtime president of the Bank of Arizona and, it is widely believed, Arizona's first millionaire. Still more crucial, Wells owned an enduring reputation of unwavering integrity. Except for some over-the-top elements in his story, no tangible reason existed to not take Wells's version of the story at face value.

Wells's account assigns the setting for the initial incident of the abandonment of the baby to an actual Whiskey Row saloon called Cob Web Hall and its ownership to the magnetic Captain "P.M." Fisher. Citing no actual date, Wells simply notes that it was a snowy winter night, and the "Cobweb" offered a warm haven. The gambling tables had been bustling, but activities were tapering off. Drinks and cigars had been sold by the gallon and bushel, but the smoke was starting to clear. The cantina's popular female vocalist had retired for the night, as had many others.

Some soldiers from Fort Whipple and miners from the nearby mountains were stretching the evening out a tad longer. A few of Captain Fisher's friends remained, including two Prescott icons, Colonel Henry Bigelow of the Nifty Saloon and Bigelow's best friend, Prescott's original surveyor, Robert Groom. They were amid a group who were lagging behind in the hopes of engaging Fisher socially. It was then that the tone of the night suddenly transmuted.

In Edmund Wells's version of the baby on the bar story, Cob Web Hall was said to be the site of events. *Sharlot Hall Museum.*

Someone noticed a peculiar bundle on the part of the bar counter that was closest to the entrance, and it was peculiar because it was moving. A sound, although stifled, was coming from it. Until that moment, no one had seen the bundle, knew how it arrived or how long it had been there. Bigelow summoned Fisher, who unraveled the parcel to discover a beautiful, ebony-eyed baby girl. He held her aloft for all to see. Some grizzled miners were dumbstruck, but the majority extended a hearty welcome. It did not take long for all to comprehend that she had been abandoned.

Suddenly, the newly homeless baby was declared up for adoption. Arguments commenced regarding the baby's immediate and future welfare. Soldiers and miners proffered their respective cases to be her adopter. Dissension started to radiate throughout the saloon.

Before the situation got out of control, Fisher interjected a proposal. All those who were desirous of adopting the child, he submitted, should partake in a game of dice: ten dollars for one throw of four dice for the pretty stranger. All of the money pooled would go to the winner to jumpstart the child's long-term care. No one dissented. After all, the Whiskey Row way of life embraced gambling.

Player after player rolled. Finally, it came time for the most unlikely candidate for parenthood to play: the aged bachelor Robert Groom. Incredibly, he laid out four fives, and with that, Groom declared himself the winner.

However, patiently waiting in the wings for his turn was Judge Charley Hall. He announced that nothing was decided yet, as he had the last throw. Excitement akin to that experienced in overtime at a sporting event filled the room as Hall braced for the roll.

The dramatic moment resulted in a miraculous throw of four sixes.

Hall had won the baby. Joyous congratulations and applause came from all but the suspicious Groom. He claimed that Hall had somehow loaded the dice. Yet Groom conceded, but with one stipulation: he must name the baby. The judge consented immediately.

The speech Wells attributed to Groom is worthy of being quoted in full. Lifting his glass of champagne, he toasted:

> *As the bead of this sparkling wine ascends to the surface, so may the destiny of this little waif rise from obscurity and sparkle amongst the stars of the heaven on earth, uplifting humanity making us better men and better women. And in memory of this presence, I now christen thee, little miss, and name thee Chance Cobweb Hall. Drink.*

Now, the judge faced the matter of telling Mrs. Hall the improbable story of how it came to pass that he was bringing a baby home for keeps. As Mrs. Hall held the child, trepidation shook her voice when she asked her husband to explain. Her fears eased as she listened to his Whiskey Row story. When her husband finished, Mrs. Hall announced, "Let us give it the best care our meager fortune will provide." The couple agreed to adopt the baby.

It was convenient that the couple's last name was "Hall," so Groom's christening needed no surname change.

Wells maintained that several fruitless attempts were made to locate the child's birth parents. Nonetheless, Mrs. Hall soon learned how the baby wound up on a bar counter on Whiskey Row and who deposited her there. It was George Ah Fat, the well-known Chinese laundry proprietor, who left her. His business registry mark had been found on one of the baby's garments, which led Mrs. Hall to visit and quiz him.

Reluctantly, Ah Fat confessed that a striking woman had left the baby in his care until she was able to better her circumstances. But after some time, he concluded she was not going to return and that there had to be a more appropriate place for a girl to be raised. He believed his friend Captain Fisher would know what to do. Instead of going directly to Fisher, however, he decided to drop her off on the counter of his saloon during a cold, stormy night, then blend into the crowd. That was all Ah Fat was willing to divulge.

Soon, wrote Wells, the whole incident "was forgotten as one of the romances of the town."

Wells then fast-forwarded some twenty-five years to a time when he was in San Francisco on business. While there, he attended a benefit for "dependent girls" and found himself sitting across a table from a young couple, of which the female member was especially attractive and strangely familiar. Wells overheard them conversing about art and the philanthropic causes they believed in and concluded they were both educated and well-to-do. He avoided interrupting, but curiosity overtook him after he heard mention of Prescott.

Wells began to informally interview the gentlewoman and learned that she had indeed been born and raised in Prescott, Arizona, but landed in California after her father, Judge Charles Hall, sent her to Mills College in Oakland. Her name? C.C. Hall, short for Chance Cobweb Hall. How she received her unusual name, her father never told her. "I suppose that some kind of western romance was connected to it. Perhaps I will know sometime."

With that, Wells ended his Chance Cobweb Hall chronicle.

The True Story of Violet "Baby Bell" Hicks

Rewinding to the night of Monday, January 17, 1898, the hot national topic was whether the United States should become militarily involved in the Cuban struggle for independence from Spanish rule. Bucky O'Neill was Prescott's mayor and just seven months away from striding fearlessly into immortality as a Rough Rider in the Spanish-American War. Locally, people were still talking about a daring robbery that had transpired at the Palace Saloon in the early morning of January 9. An eight-month-old girl, however, was about to become "the sensation of the season."

As Wells asserted, it was indeed an exceptionally cold, snowy night, and the saloons of Whiskey Row offered comfortable retreats. Cob Web Hall, which was indeed still alive and well on the Row, was probably as busy as any other saloon on the Row. But there would not be a baby placed on its bar that night. That distinction would belong to the Cabinet Saloon.

Although he had been the proprietor of the Cob Web in the 1880s, Captain Fisher was not at the Cabinet or any other cantina that night. He had died almost exactly nine years before. Colonel Bigelow was also certainly absent, as he had died in 1892. Theoretically, it is possible Robert Groom was present. Although he resided in Wickenburg during this time, he frequently visited Prescott while checking on nearby mines he owned. It is doubtful, however, that the seventy-three-year-old bachelor would have wanted to adopt and raise a baby.

Robert Groom was seventy-three years old when Baby Bell was abandoned on a Whiskey Row saloon bar. *Sharlot Hall Museum.*

The Cabinet was now being run by coproprietors Ben Belcher and Barney Smith. Contrary to Wells's attestation, the night was not winding down. The clamor inherent to saloon life was at a fever pitch. A high-stakes faro game was still attracting the attention of many Cabinet patrons, and the soprano who was said to have retired for the night in Wells's rendering was, according to the *Miner*, still "hold[ing] sway on the stage at the rear of the saloon." Amid this civilized commotion, if anyone wanted to accomplish something surreptitious, now was the time.

There are no references to Belcher or Smith being present that night. It was their "genial mixologist" Frank Williams running the show—he plays counterpart to Captain Fisher of Wells's version. Naturally, he was keeping an eye on the Cabinet's bat-winged doors. His attention piqued when "a rather comely young woman" wearing a veil walked through them. But there was more—she was holding a swaddled baby.

The mysterious lady laid the bundle down along with a note on the bar counter and said something unintelligible to Williams. While making her getaway, the stunned bartender called out to her, "[W]hat does this all mean?" but she quickly disappeared into the darkness of Whiskey Row. A few nearby witnesses were moved when the child responded to his voice by extending a tiny hand and cooing as if to say, "Be my friend and shake." Fatherly instinct seized Williams; he rushed out in search of nourishment for the cherub.

Meanwhile, all peripheral activities ceased; the precious waif magnetized everyone present. The baby's gender wasn't yet known, but the consensus was that it was a girl—and an exceptionally beautiful one. All were bewildered by her presence.

Hence, another Cabinet employee stood above the crowd to clarify the situation by reading the note left behind, quoted here verbatim:

> *Mr. Saloon Keeper, Dear Sir—Here is a baby that belongs to William Bell, and he has left it on an invalid woman who has no one to do anything for her and is at this time sick in bed and his child is suffering for care, and she has sent it down here to its father, hearing that he was there at your saloon of nights; and will you be so kind as to give the child in his hands or give it to the sheriff, for the woman is not able to keep the child nor cannot do it if he was paying her, but he does nothing for it.*

Western saloon stories often result in drunken men pulling pistols and shooting at each other, but this tale is of a more heartwarming variety. The *Courier* reported that "a surging mass of brawny men crowded up to get a sight of the little one." No less than forty were so taken with the infant—and undoubtedly inflicted with a benevolence supercharged by whiskey—that they volunteered to give it a home. A few married but childless men were even on the brink of fisticuffing for the tiny trophy. Things were getting out of control, so someone left to fetch Charles Hicks (not Hall), the probate judge of Yavapai County.

It is immediately clear that Hicks was not at the Cabinet when the baby was placed on the bar. One report conveyed that bartender Williams cared for the baby "until the arrival of Judge Hicks." In other words, he was not already there, waiting to gamble for possession of the child. The most

Eight-month-old Violet Bell was deposited on this bar in the Cabinet Saloon on January 17, 1898. *Sharlot Hall Museum.*

Charles Hicks, a probate judge of Prescott, removed Baby Bell from the Cabinet Saloon and eventually adopted her with his wife, Allie. *Sharlot Hall Museum.*

trustworthy initial report, which came from the *Courier*, tersely stated that at some point, Hicks "finally captured the cherub and sent it home."

Were men gambling for the right to adopt Baby Bell when Judge Hicks arrived? Evidence suggests that although they might not have been gambling to adopt Violet, they were indeed gambling and anteing money "for the child's benefit." Two outside reports indicate that Hicks took not only the baby with him but $300. Charity on Whiskey Row was not uncommon.

Ten days later, the *Miner* iterated that the judge had indeed not only "been sent for," but after appearing, "decided the question by announcing that he would take it himself." A refutation of Wells's assertion that the baby was an absolute stranger also appeared in the initial *Courier* report, citing that Hicks took it "home to its grandmother residing in West Prescott." The grandmother refused the child and provided some alibis for her daughter; hence, the judge took the baby home to his wife, Allie.

What is known about the January 17 portion of this story ends there.

Wells claimed the baby's biological parents were never known. In truth, the father, William Bell, was identified immediately by the note left at the Cabinet. This made it easy to identify the mother, Mary Bell. Rumors swirled regarding her whereabouts. One rumor was that she had been sick in the county hospital but had returned to Jerome to work, leaving her baby with her mother, Mrs. Harvey, in west Prescott. More likely, Mary and Violet had been living with her mother all along, but Mary was now in hiding.

William Bell had indeed been seen frequenting the Cabinet "for some weeks" and had probably been there that day   he had been seen in town. He may have been at the Cabinet the very night and moment his child was left on the saloon's bar counter. At any rate, he learned of the incident and skipped town. A warrant for his arrest was immediately issued. The public learned on January 26 that "Wm. Bell, of Baby Bell fame, was brought in from Crown King yesterday and lodged in jail."

Meanwhile, the Hickses were enjoying their new guest. According to the judge, "Baby Bell is one of the best babies in the country." He also divulged to the public the little one's gender for the first time: "She never cries at night, and she is good all day long."

The Hickses' bliss was interrupted when an unexpected visitor showed up at their door on January 26. It was Mary Bell, accompanied by her sister, who claimed she had come down from Jerome. She told the Hickses, probably after visiting William in jail, that neither she nor her husband desired to give up their daughter. As distressing as this must have been for Mr. and Mrs. Hicks, they held their ground; they were not willing to release the girl to either of her abandoners.

The *Miner* was pleased to report that "Baby Bell will continue to remain an interesting occupant of the Hicks household for the present." Yet the child's future now seemed more in limbo than the couple had hoped. To combat this, the judge shared a deleterious revelation about her mother: "She did not ask to see her progeny." On this day, most likely after Mary Bell's visit, Allie Hicks hurriedly petitioned for the adoption of Violet Bell.

On January 28, William and Mary Bell and Mrs. Harvey stood before Justice Donald Campbell. It was Mr. Bell, however, who was actually on trial for failing to support his wife and daughter. Bell's defense was that he was jobless and having trouble finding work, but while working, he supported them. He then asserted he cared for his daughter while also admitting he'd been away for months and contributed nothing toward her welfare.

Bell's profession of paternal love was discounted by an eyewitness to the trial: "[H]is bearing was rather defiant, his tone and manner indicating that he felt like breaking out and had to struggle to control himself." This same onlooker questioned Bell's claim he could not find work, noting he was "a robust-looking man of about thirty-five years of age."

Campbell refused all excuses and gave Bell twenty-five days in jail.

Mary Bell—not appearing invalid as the note stated—was given every benefit of the doubt. No longer speaking on her estranged husband's behalf, she retracted, or at least clarified, half of what she had told the Hickses and contradicted what was declared in the note left behind at the Cabinet. Mrs. Bell now testified that she expected financial support from Mr. Bell for the child only and nothing more. This may have been enough to free her of abandonment charges but not her expressed desire to reclaim custody of her baby girl; the court was not convinced.

That same day, the Bells signed over their daughter to the Hickses. Violet Bell was now Violet Hicks. There can be little doubt that the adoption of Baby Bell was expedited because Charles Hicks was the probate judge of Yavapai County; probate judges handled all adoptions at this time in territorial history. Even more critical, both William and Mary Bell had abandoned their daughter, albeit in different ways. Mary Bell had dealt a hand against herself by allowing someone—or doing so herself—to deposit her baby on a saloon counter and leaving, or at least endorsing, a note that relinquished her role as mother.

All in all, locals believed the adoption was for the best. The *Courier*, while also revealing the child's first name for the first time, stated, "Thus has the little waif of the Cabinet Saloon fallen into a home good enough for any child, one in which she will receive that care, training and education which any parents would be proud to have a child receive."

And thus ended the public drama of Violet "Baby Bell" Hicks. Judge Wells's statement that it "was forgotten as one of the romances of the town" is true in the sense that it disappeared from Prescott media.

Of the many questions spawning from the night of January 17, 1898, the most intriguing is: Who was the mysterious lady who dropped Baby Bell off at the Cabinet Saloon? Only two suspects emerge: Mary Bell herself and her sister. The *Courier* referred to the person who deposited the baby on the saloon counter as a "rather comely young woman." Later, that same paper reported after the trial that Mrs. Bell was also not only "rather good looking" but "appear[ed] to be about twenty years of age." It was clear what the *Courier* was inferring.

Mary claimed she had been sick when the baby was left on the Cabinet Saloon bar and afterward said that she had traveled to Jerome to work and then come back to Prescott. Given the tight chronology of events between January 17 and January 26, when Mary Bell visited the Hicks household, it appears likely these were simply alibis to avoid abandonment charges. Mary Bell surfaces as the most likely malefactor.

Very little is known about Violet Hicks's childhood. She revealed a bare minimum to her children about her past. Her son Chester Binner, the youngest of her four children, remembered his mother sharing that she had learned to ride a horse before she could walk. He said she had also been fond of a Chinese cook who resided in the Hickses' household. That was about it. Chester, although he knew his mother was adopted, did not learn about the Cabinet Saloon incident of January 17, 1898, until 1999, when he was interviewed by writer/historian Leo Banks for a chapter in one of his books.

Sadly, Violet never got to know her adoptive mother. Allie Hicks died on February 7, 1900.

Violet Hicks never knew her adopted mother, Allie, who died in early 1900 and was buried in Prescott's Odd Fellows Cemetery. *Norman Fisk.*

In 1972, a pulp western history magazine called *Frontier Times* spoke of rumors that C.C. Hall, under an assumed name, was living anonymously in the shadows of Whiskey Row. This was never true.

Violet's adult life was far less magic than it was tragic.

At some point, Violet moved to California, just as Wells said. There is no record that she ever attended Mills College, an all-girls school, as Wells claimed, but she did attend an art school in San Francisco. There, she met her future husband, Arthur Binner Jr., who would become a successful architectural sculptor. Early in their marriage, they lived in Oakland. For a while, they were happy together with their four children; Violet's son even remarked that she was "a great mother in my early life." Wells's implication that she was doing well in early adulthood seems to ring true.

But things began to unravel when Arthur started drinking. By the time Chester turned four years old, Arthur began beating Violet and became abusive, even to the extent of expressing murderous intentions toward his children. At some point in 1929, Violet obtained a restraining order.

Arthur then cut off financial support. Her adopted father visited her around this time and stayed for several weeks, surely to try to improve his beloved daughter's situation, as he had always done. This was the last time they were together.

Charles Hicks died on Christmas Eve 1929, shortly after his visit with Violet. His adopted daughter attended his funeral in Prescott. Violet's son recalled that his mother believed her worries were over after learning the former judge had owned some gold mines. She thought she'd receive a sizable inheritance. Chester explained, however, that Hicks had not "[kept] up the assay payments or something, and [Violet] didn't get any inheritance at all. [S]he came back home disgusted."

After her husband left and Charles Hicks passed, Violet became not only sad and bitter but also a gambling addict. Chester professed that his mother spent a lot of time at the racetrack: "[W]hen she won, she took us to the circus, and when she lost, the landlord was pounding on the door." There were times, he recalled, when there was nothing more to eat than a single onion.

Violet was able to reconnect with her biological mother, Mary Bell, and establish a good relationship. Sadly, after trekking all the way to Alaska to find her father, William Bell, she was informed he wanted nothing to do with her. His abandonment was total.

Although, in another manner, Violet became a deserter of her progeny as well, kicking Chester out of the house when he was seventeen because she could no longer feed him. She died in 1970 at the age of seventy-two. Chester didn't learn of her death until months later.

Why are there so many differences between Edmund Wells's Chance Cobweb Hall saga and the true story of Violet Hicks? Was it simply a case of an eighty-something-year-old man confusing and/or forgetting the facts? The answer is most certainly not. *Argonaut Tales* is too well-written, too lucid, creative and, at times, philosophical. The mind that penned it was clearly operating at a high level.

There is enough evidence to make an inference that Wells knew the true story of Violet Hicks and purposely altered it. First, Wells and Charles Hicks were well acquainted and had probably even been close friends. When a young Charles Hicks first arrived in the Prescott area in 1880, his first employer was none other than Edmund Wells. Also, both were judges.

It is not difficult to deduce that Wells, in the interest of protecting his friend and his friend's family, may have camouflaged the true story. Indeed, being abandoned by both biological parents could have an adverse psychological effect on an individual—not to mention knowing that the story included being coldly deposited on a frontier town saloon counter most likely by her own mother.

It is possible Violet never knew how she had come to be adopted. Chester, when he was a much older man, said neither he nor Violet's other children ever knew their mother was Whiskey Row's famous "baby on the bar." Indeed, even Wells's "C.C. Hall" character never knew the origin of her name.

Interestingly, there was a well-known traveling businessman from Albuquerque who often visited Prescott. His name was C.C. Hall. Was Wells communicating an inside joke with Prescottonians by using that name in *Argonaut Tales*?

For serious historians or those who simply love to hear and/or read history, it's important to acknowledge there is a place for legend and folklore, popular history, anti-footnoters and historical fiction. They make the truly curious seek true, scholarship-oriented history.

It is human nature to try to make something beautiful out of something that is not so beautiful. Addressing this matter, an overall warning regarding *Argonaut Tales* was issued by none other than one of Arizona's most celebrated poets and historians, Sharlot Hall. In a review of Wells's book before it was released to the general public, she cautioned future readers: "It is not all history, not meant to be all history." Then to substantiate the value of literature similar to *Argonaut Tales*, she added, "The pages that are pure romance are perhaps more true and valuable than the ones that are history verified—just as a man's dreams are more true and permanently valuable than his everyday life."

It is equally human to dig deep for historical truth, knowing that, while it might not be what was hoped for, it is still a treasure trove from which to learn.

The most obvious lesson extracted from the Violet "Baby Bell" Hicks story is that abandonment by one's biological parents is a formidable psychological hurdle to overcome, even after experiencing a special love from adoptive parents.

The true history of Violet Bell, also known as Violet Hicks and finally Violet Binner, is one that began with a turmoil she was too young to remember. Yet it led to a childhood whereby she experienced advantages many children of her time might not have. As an adult, she reverted to domestic chaos and a personal life marked by sadness and bitterness.

If a modern-day movie was made of this story, the legend of Chance Cobweb Hall would prove the better choice. Yet we would miss the lessons that can be learned from reality. Sometimes, however, it is good to have both—the truth and the favored illusion.

13

TRUE TALES FROM PRESCOTT'S GREAT FIRE OF 1900

By Bradley G. Courtney

Prescott's Great Fire of 1900 was the most pivotal event in the town's history. Two-thirds of Prescott's business district was destroyed. The monetary loss was staggering: an estimated $1.5 million—almost $50 million in today's currency. After Prescott burned, some amusing, inspiring and fascinating true tales emerged over the years, as those who witnessed the Great Fire gathered and shared their stories.

Harry Brisley, a pharmacist who owned two downtown drugstores that burned to the ground, was an eyewitness to most, if not all, of the Great Fire. He wrote of an incident that transpired during the earliest stages of the fiery nightmare.

There "occurred a scene worthy of a western movie thriller around the corner of Gurley and Cortez Streets, hastening from another duty was the city engineer and his familiar wagon, grievously belaboring his old white horse. Thence sharply turning into the corner of Gurley and South Montezuma, they together continued their fevered race toward the reservoir," Brisley wrote many years after the Great Fire. This heroic figure was John Love, Prescott's city water engineer.

Absent from accounts of the Great Fire of 1900 is an astounding revelation that may have been kept quiet for years. Water was available early on to fight the fire, but it was not discovered until near the end of the conflagration. According to Bill Fitzgerald, after reaching the reservoir, Love started the pumps and sent ample water to the water mains and hydrants. However,

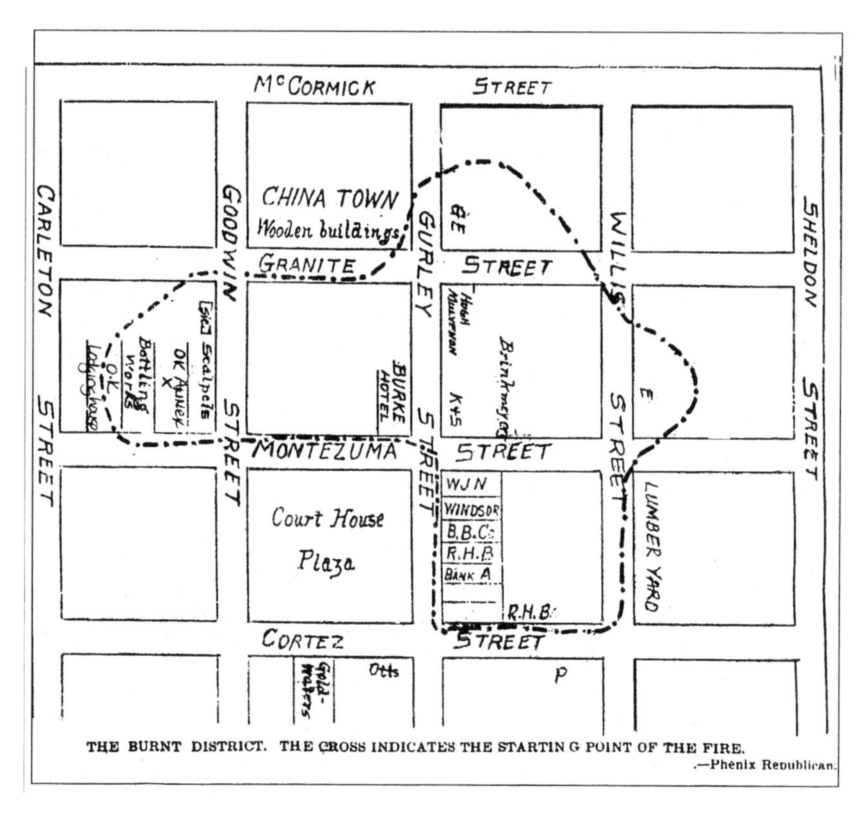

THE BURNT DISTRICT. THE CROSS INDICATES THE STARTING POINT OF THE FIRE. —Phenix Republican.

With a few errors, this map shows the general area that burned down during Prescott's Great Fire of 1900. *Bradley G. Courtney.*

While most of Prescott's downtown area was burning, those who were fighting the fire were unaware that ample water had been sent down into the mains. *Sharlot Hall Museum.*

after initially receiving insufficient water from the hydrants and wells—and in their desperation to find other means with which to fight the fire—the fresh supply went unnoticed until after the majority of the damage had been done. Love remained at the reservoir for the duration of the fire, awaiting instructions that never came.

DAGO MARTIN'S CLOSE CALL

When it was thought there was no water in the mains and that the wells on each corner of the Plaza were almost totally dry, those fighting the fire resorted to dynamiting buildings in the fire's path in the hopes of stopping it in its tracks. One the first targets was the Union Saloon—part saloon but mostly brothel—on the northeast corner of Goodwin and Granite Streets.

Dago Martin was hustling about in the cellar of the Union Saloon, hoping to save some of the cases of booze that were stored down there. Unaware of Martin's presence in the basement, the firefighters hurled a cache of dynamite into the middle of the saloon. Suddenly, the building above Martin disappeared, and he found himself staring up into a night sky brightened by the flames. Martin was nearly deaf for more than two weeks, but he thought it was a miracle that he lived through the experience.

The Union Saloon was part-saloon but was mainly a brothel. *Sharlot Hall Museum.*

The Union Saloon was one of the many businesses that was dynamited in the hopes of stopping the fire during the evening of July 14, 1900. *Sharlot Hall Museum.*

CHINATOWN IS SAVED

When the ingenious residents of Prescott's Chinatown on South Granite Street and the east bank of Granite Creek saw the fire moving their way, they grabbed quilts and cushions, placed them on the roofs of their houses and businesses and soaked them with water they had hauled and stored from the creek. They watched as flying embers landed on rooftops and lit up surrounding buildings. Several images taken after the Great Fire reveal that the flames circumvented the Chinese quarters.

The only damage reported in Chinatown was that a Qing Dynasty dragon flag atop the joss house, a sacred meeting place to the Chinese, was burned. It was finally replaced on August 17. This riled up a few local American patriots. A group of them marched over to the Chinese quarters and demanded that an American flag be placed above the Chinese pennant. A heated parley followed. The Chinese residents eventually agreed to the demand. Soon, one man surfaced with an American flag that was a full six inches long and four inches wide. The Chinese banner was hauled down, the little American flag placed above it, and both were run to the top of the pole. In the end, everyone got a chuckle out of it.

Prescott before the Great Fire of 1900. Chinatown can be seen toward the bottom of this image. *Sharlot Hall Museum.*

There were many close calls. One occurred near Granite Creek, where a powder house, a shed holding one thousand pounds of blasting powder, was located. A freelancer known as Tommy was spotted by two firemen crawling "crab-fashion" from underneath it. When asked, "What the hell are you doing?" Tommy, not knowing what was in the shed, said that he had placed five sticks of dynamite underneath it and lit the fuse with the idea of preventing the flames from reaching Prescott's west side. The two heroic firefighters dived underneath and pulled the fuse out in the nick of time, saving the shack, Chinatown and west Prescott.

PRESCOTTONIANS SING AN APROPOS SONG WHILE THEIR TOWN BURNED

Twenty-five years after the fire, firefighter Bob Morrison recalled that a group of men carried the piano from the Palace Saloon onto the Plaza. Ed Wilson, the Palace pianist who was probably a member of that group, was followed by a singer described as a "painted lady." When the piano was situated properly, Wilson sat down and started hammering out a popular song of that day, the appropriately inappropriate "There'll Be a Hot Time in the Old Town Tonight," while the saloon girl sang heartily, and the fire destroyed businesses across the street.

Evidence indicates that this is more than just a good story. The testimony of William Greenwood, an eyewitness to the fire, an employee of Sam Hill's Hardware and formerly one of Theodore Roosevelt's Rough Riders, confirmed, "Even a piano was moved to the new location, and soon, someone was playing 'There'll Be a Hot Time in the Old Town Tonight.'"

The song caught on and was sung several times. At one point, people from as far away as Granite Street could be heard singing along as the roar of the fire moved east, and soon, seemingly half the town joined in. One report claimed that during one of Wilson's renditions, when he reached the chorus, another dynamite explosion from a nearby building caused an iron bar to be hurled in his direction. Luckily, it flew directly over his head and smashed into a hose cart.

Perhaps the most famous story regarding the Great Fire is that of Palace patrons carrying the saloon's bar across the street to the Plaza. For many years, local historians and Palace proprietors and enthusiasts have sparred over whether this legend is true. Indeed, no contemporaneous reports of that event exist. However, a little detective work and some recently discovered research material puts an end to that dispute.

THE LEGEND OF THE PALACE BAR

Prior to the release of The History Press's *Prescott's Original Whiskey Row* in November 2015, there had been some debate (sometimes heated) between local historians and Whiskey Row businessowners and regulars about whether what is perhaps Prescott's most famous and cherished legend is true—that is, the story of Palace patrons pulling the saloon's bar, the same bar sitting in the Palace today, out to the Plaza while the inferno was racing north up Montezuma Street.

Several sincere and legitimate local historians concluded that it is nothing more than fiction—and for good reason. It has been thought by some that such an incident would surely have been reported around the time that it happened if it did indeed happen. What is probably true is that the event did not seem newsworthy at the time. Thousands of items were pulled out to the Plaza during the Great Fire. Why report this one? The Palace's bar was no more important than any other rescued article at

The original Palace Saloon (*last building to the left*) was established on Goodwin Street before it was burned downed in 1884 and relocated to Montezuma Street. *Sharlot Hall Museum.*

that time, and surely, it was not the only bar pulled out. Furthermore, no one could have predicted that the Palace Restaurant and Saloon would become what it has become today—or that the event would even matter more than one hundred years later.

The story has been passed down through oral history. This has rendered doubt in some minds not only because oral history changes a story the more it is told, but there is also no actual written documentation to prove the legend's veracity. Recent evidence leaves no room for doubt. But it requires a deeper dive into the history of the celebrated Palace bar.

From 1884 to late 1897, the Palace's bar was made of solid walnut, unlike the bar featured in today's Palace. However, around six o'clock on the evening of Friday, November 5, 1897, a "lurid glare" was seen from one of the windows of the Palace Saloon. Like so many times before along Whiskey Row, shouts of "Fire!" were heard. This fire would test the Palace's brick, stone and iron construction.

The source of the 1897 fire was a broken pipe above the steak fryer in the kitchen. The fire gained impetus, and flames burst through the popular saloon's front windows, shattering glass and electric light rondures. The firemen arrived with a swiftness that was compared to that of fire departments in larger cities. They quickly extinguished the flames.

The interior of the Palace was badly damaged, but the brick, stone and iron did the jobs they were expected to do and contained the fire. If the Palace had not been fashioned from these materials in 1884, a repeat of the 1883 Whiskey Row fire, when flames quickly spread to neighboring buildings

The Palace Saloon on Montezuma Street. Its stone, brick and iron saved the rest of Whiskey Row in 1897 after a fire broke out inside. *Sharlot Hall Museum.*

would have ensued. The full story of the Whiskey Row fire of 1883 is told in *Prescott's Original Whiskey Row*.

The wooden portions in the saloon area were either burned to a crisp or badly damaged. The *Miner* stated, "The front end of one of the most handsomely finished and best-appointed saloons in Arizona presented a charred mass of ruins, while the water stood six inches on the floor."

Of great significance, the solid walnut bar, which was fitted after the Palace Saloon was moved from Goodwin Street to Montezuma Street in 1884, was destroyed. It had to be replaced. The total damages were estimated to cost $5,000, almost $160,000 today. Insurance arrived promptly, and the proprietor Bob Brow began rebuilding.

Requiring only fifty-three days to restructure, the Palace reopened on December 28. It was a festive event. A brass band welcomed a throng that agreed the new Palace was a work of art: "Everything about the place betokens both elegance and taste," read the *Miner*.

Some notable changes had been made. First, the Palace's restaurant and dining section had been moved to the rear, making them separate from the saloon. A side entrance to the dining area was created so that, according to the *Miner*, "ladies who objected to entering a saloon may be properly served."

Second, a new bar was installed, and it most likely came by train from a Brunswick, Balke and Collender store in San Francisco. The *Miner*'s description of the bar is historically significant, as it offers proof that it was the same bar that people were leaning on and enjoying a drink at on July

The only known image of the interior of the Palace Saloon before the Great Fire of 1900, clearly showing the bar was present then. *Sharlot Hall Museum.*

The Palace bar could possibly be under this stack of rescued items—seen in lower center here. *Sharlot Hall Museum.*

A section of the Palace's famous bar could be seen in the temporary saloon that sat on Prescott's Plaza as the town was being rebuilt. *Sharlot Hall Museum.*

The Palace's pre–Great Fire of 1900 bar was reinstalled in 1901, after being saved from the flames. *Sharlot Hall Museum.*

Today, the famous Palace bar is photographed by visitors on a daily basis. *Norman Fisk.*

14, 1900. It stated, "The new bar is one of the handsomest in the southwest. It is made of cherry and is massive in proportions and finished in the most elaborate and artistic style." A perfect match.

This report and photographic evidence prove that this was the same Palace bar that was being used when the Great Fire of 1900 struck Whiskey Row; it is plainly seen in the only known pre–Great Fire image of the Palace's interior, featured on this page (made red for designers). Additionally, a section of it is visible in one of the best-known photographs taken shortly after the fire, that of "BROW'S PALACE AND NOT ASHAMED OF IT," taken on the Plaza in Brow's temporary makeshift saloon after the fire.

The legend of this now-famous piece of furniture being saved during the Great Fire has been proven true. Ideas vary as to exactly how this was achieved. Some say men hooked horses to the bar and dragged it out. Oxen have been credited with the same—as have men. It was probably carried out by determined and loyal Palace patrons fueled by whiskey-fed courage.

The celebrated bar is still in the Palace today and is photographed by visitors on a daily basis.

The Boy Heroes of East Prescott

Perhaps the most endearing episode that occurred during the Great Fire was that of two young boys who became the heroes of east Prescott. While flames were gobbling the buildings that faced the Plaza on Gurley Street, the fire began racing eastward toward Cortez Street. The west side of Cortez Street was often considered an extension of Whiskey Row, as it was the home of several saloons. The east side of Cortez Street, however, had been known as "Office Row," even though Whiskey Row existed at the same time. In the past, Prescottonians were prouder of Office Row than Whiskey Row, because whiskey had been the source of so many problems and unplanned crimes. Hence, the name was left out of print until most of it burned down in 1883.

If the fire continued to behave as it had for the previous nearly three hours, Office Row appeared to be next on its list of victims.

At the junction of Gurley and Cortez Streets, a one-hundred-man bucket brigade formed. It is likely that someone finally discovered the water that had previously released into the mains by city water engineer John Love. On the northeast corner stood the Bellevue House, where two unidentified boys climbed onto its roof. Because soaring embers were creating so much havoc, the bucket brigade men instructed the lads to douse any embers that landed on Office Row roofs with the buckets of water they hoisted up to them. If a bucket was not available, the nimble boys were to kick the embers to the street. They energetically did this for at least an hour—perhaps longer.

Some people believed the boys' efforts saved as much as ten blocks of east Prescott, although that is probably an exaggeration. Nonetheless, the fire did not cross Cortez Street, and the unnamed heroic boys played a large part in preventing that from happening. Both received minor burns.

Harry Brisley noted, "It was reported that Brow, Belcher and Smith of the Palace [and Cabinet] had tapped kegs of cold beer nearby the courthouse and was free to all comers. Never had been heard more welcome news after five hours of continuous toil." Much to their disappointment, the two courageous boys were told they were not invited to this party but should go on home and rest. The soot-covered heroes sauntered home. Their rites of passage would have to wait.

14

PRESCOTT'S PLAZA WAS THE CENTER OF TOWN LIFE

By Drew Desmond

When, in 1864, Robert Groom plotted out Prescott and created the Plaza in the middle of downtown, it was not initially meant for the county courthouse. The first courthouse was located on the street facing the Plaza, and the Plaza was left as an open public space. Its uses were many and varied.

The first community use of the Plaza was the Fourth of July celebration in 1864. On July 2, a flagpole standing fourteen and a half stories tall was erected "in the southeast corner [across from the present downtown post office] of the Plaza," the *Miner* described. On July 4, "the Stars and Stripes were first thrown to the breeze.…Prescott was only thirty-five days old, born at the May 30th meeting of Governor Goodwin and his staff." It was estimated that four hundred men, mostly miners, came into town to celebrate.

A month later, an artesian well was successfully dug on the Plaza, providing fresh water for those in need. By September, the *Miner* reported that "fruit is beginning to become quite plentiful. We see the Plaza full of boys selling apricots."

In Prescott's earliest days, lodging was both scarce and expensive. Many travelers simply pitched camp in the Plaza during their visits and were welcome to do so.

In its early days, the Plaza was often the site of baseball games. One match pitted the boys from Prescott against a strong, well-practiced team from the Verde Valley. Verde won the lopsided contest by the ridiculous score of 66 to

27. The outfield must have been located toward the north side of the Plaza. When one of the Verde boys clubbed the ball especially hard, the paper cracked that it must have landed "in Sam Miller's meadow" (Miller Valley today). In another "match" game on the Plaza, an "all-star" team called the Prescott Champions faced off against the boys from Fort Whipple. Whipple won that contest 47 to 21. The hometown paper lamented that Prescott simply had to spend more time practicing.

In March 1867, the public place was nearly purloined. "We are sorry to announce the arrival of the notorious and vagabond called 'squatter' in our devoted town…but it appears, from some mysterious cause, a party of men, mostly strangers in our country, have deliberately located or 'jumped' our town plaza and are now proceeding to take and fence it in," the paper proclaimed.

The plot brought both disgust and consternation. Eighty-four prominent citizens signed a petition that demanded the jumpers "desist from further operations."

"We will once again proffer a word of advice to the jumpers," the paper wrote. "Take your post and rails to some other locality, where, if you desire to cultivate ground, you can get a legitimate title to it for a mere trifle—not one-quarter the cost of litigation which is sure to follow your recent operation." Indeed, litigation did follow, which Prescott happily won. By December, the last remains of the squatters' "improvements" were hauled away.

From the late 1860s to the early 1870s, people were allowed to plant personal gardens in the Plaza. The documented crops included watermelon and corn. "The patch of corn growing in Judge Berry's garden on the east side of the Plaza is worth looking at; it is so tall and vigorous," the *Miner* declared. Considering the corn endured three frosts, the paper attributed the judge's success to his constant weeding.

Band concerts were a regular feature of the Plaza and most often included Fort Whipple's band. Indeed, these concerts were so popular that by 1875, a bandstand was constructed in the Plaza. This fixture still exists on the Plaza, although people call it the gazebo today.

The first grass planted on the Plaza was placed there by Bucky O'Neill when he received one hundred pounds of Bermuda grass from the Department of Agriculture in April 1890.

Two years later, it was put to good use when "permission [was] given the Lawn Tennis Club…to use a section of ground on the southeast corner of the Plaza," the *Miner* related. "Deputy Recorder Tritle is looking joyously ahead to the opening of the lawn tennis grounds on the Plaza, when a fine form beckoned in a neat striped suit of regulation tennis clothes will be

Prescott's bandstand (or gazebo) as it appears today. *Drew Desmond.*

shown to great advantage." Lawn tennis was quite popular in Prescott, with a club that was already well established in 1887. The sport also doubled as a social mixer. The newspaper explained that the game "provide[d] some source of amusement for the social enjoyment of our young men and maidens. The game of lawn tennis has met with remarkable success in the East, being beyond doubt the most popular of all outdoor sports, enjoyed alike by both sexes."

The second or "Old Courthouse" took center stage when it was built in 1878 and people began referring to the public area as the "Courthouse Plaza." Although some have mistakenly taken to calling the rectangular plaza "the square," it was never called that in the past.

The Plaza was also where one could find Prescott's community pets.

OLD JOE: PRESCOTT'S BELOVED FIRE HORSE

On March 6, 1906, Joe was purchased to be a fire horse. He was seven years old and almost at once dropped into the correct spirit of a firefighting horse. He became the pet of every fireman who ever knew him.

"Old Joe was a registered draft horse and was a real, sure enough horse," the *Miner* contended. "He was credited with more real 'horse sense' than many young recruits in the fire department." Joe was the perfect fire horse. Whenever he heard the fire alarm, he was ready to bolt at full speed. "He stood his ground at many a dangerous and smoky ruin, waiting the command of his driver as if he would sacrifice his life rather than move against orders in a crisis." Old Joe's popularity was due, in part, to his entertaining showmanship. "He would kneel down and say his prayers with you," his driver said. "He would shake hands and could count his age correctly by pawing the earth the correct number of times and many other impromptu stunts."

Joe served faithfully and outstandingly, but eventually, age began to catch up with him. "He was a special favorite of all the chiefs, and they were half sick when he had to be taken away on account of being crippled in an accident and on account of increasing age and as well as the coming of the gasoline fire wagons," the *Miner* reported. Despite this malady, the city kept Old Joe and gave him duty on the garbage wagon, where he "did good service up until" he passed away. He died suddenly and unexpectedly. "He was unharnessed as usual [one day] and seemed alright, but later in the evening, [he] took sick and died a few hours later," the paper stated.

"The boys in the fire hall are in mourning," the *Miner* related. "They have lost an old friend. It is not as if the old friend had been a schoolmate or a fellow who went swimming with them on Sundays, but just the same, it was a friend who seemed to understand them and whom they seemed to understand." One of Joe's riders testified that "he was the best educated horse he ever knew."

The big bay horse died in May 1920 at the age of twenty-one. "All the [firefighting] boys...as well as the garbage drivers, are next to heartbroken, thinking of the faithful service of Old Joe," the *Miner* observed. "They say he exemplified that great virtue in life often lacking in men: 'faithfulness to duty and willingness to work without a murmur.'"

STUB THE CAT

Stub probably would have been lost to history if it wasn't for the keen eye of researcher Michael Spencer, who noticed that the cat was included in, of all places, an inventory of the Old Courthouse.

In 1897, the Yavapai County Board of Supervisors requested the inventory. The sheriff's office, which was under George Ruffner at the time, listed one of his office's items as "1 Cat (answers to the name of Stub)." According to the *Arizona Republican*, Stub first appeared at the Old Courthouse around 1887. Although nearly all of his story is lost, the papers did mention the feline on a few occasions.

In early 1899, the *Courier* revealed that the cat was no longer answering to anything: "It has been discovered that 'Stub,' the courthouse cat, is deaf as a post. His loss of the sense of hearing is probably due to old age and eardrums worn-out from listening to legal declamations [there]." It seems that the *Courier* wasn't a big fan of the cat. The blurb continues: "'Stub' is a courthouse hanger-on of about twelve years standing, and it is about time for him to rotate out in favor of another cat."

The last mention of Stub occurred when the *Courier* and the *Miner* were editorially arguing over the issue of "free silver." The *Miner* wrote:

> *I notice, however, in the columns of the* Courier*...that the free silver idea received quite a substantial endorsement; that paper having stated that "Stub," the courthouse cat, had gathered sufficient wisdom in age to declare out for 16 to 1. There has been some doubt for a long time about where the* Courier *got some of its advanced ideas, but it was never suggested that "Stub" was being consulted.*

Nothing else is known of the feline.

MIKE THE DOG

Mike the dog crossed over the rainbow bridge on December 14, 1960. So beloved was Mike that money was raised for a small memorial plague, which still lies on the north end of the Plaza. Mike got his name from the location where he spent most of his time: Hotel St. Michael. "Just a black and white canine with dubious origins, the 'community dog' was a Whiskey Row landmark that will never be replaced," the *Courier* noted.

It was in 1946 that Mike first appeared in Prescott. Exactly how he got there is disputed. Some say a guest at St. Michael left him. Others say he came in after stowing away on the train. Others claim that when he first arrived, his paws were bloody from walking so far. Mike was an especially friendly dog who took his "duties as Prescott's unofficial host seriously in his self-assigned headquarters in front of the St. Michael Hotel each day. Mike waited for passers-by to stop and pet him and say a few friendly words. Each evening, he would retire to the lobby to greet out-of-state guests or Prescottonians arriving for their dinner meetings." Eskimo Pies were his favorite treat, although he "was rewarded with [many] handouts from bar owners and patrons....Local man Johnny Jordan would always order two steaks, one for Mike," the *Courier* noted.

"Several ranchers tried to take him home, but Mike always returned to Prescott streets and the hotel, where he lived royally on leftovers from the dining room," the *Courier* related. One resident claimed that when she was intimidated by some wild dogs downtown, Mike ran across the Plaza, barking and growling. He fought the pack's leader and drove them away. Once, Mike's territorial instincts led him to try to drive away all the seeing eye dogs that were attending a convention for the blind.

"A judge once decreed that Mike was an outlaw because he wasn't licensed. This created a dilemma, because Mike didn't belong to any one person but to the hundreds who flocked to Whiskey Row. It was resolved when local cops raised the money for the tag," the *Courier* reported. Then, one night, "employees of the hotel noticed that Mike didn't seem 'up to par.' One of Mike's vets, Dr. Horace Warner, passed the dog in the lobby, scratched his head and noticed he wasn't very chipper. Employees planned to take Mike to Warner's animal hospital [the next] morning," but instead, he was found dead at his usual post in front of the hotel.

It was requested that he be buried in the Plaza, but this request was denied, since it might start a precedent that would lead to the Plaza becoming a graveyard of sorts. Mike's final resting place is debated as much as his arrival. Some say he was buried "in a scenic spot in the Groom Creek area." Others say he was buried at a private residence near the fairgrounds.

"One man suggested that if Mike could have talked, he could have written a best-seller. 'He possessed qualities above many humans,'" he told the *Courier*. "In 1961, the pooch was memorialized by a metal plaque placed

Mike's memorial plaque on the northwest corner of the plaza. *Drew Desmond.*

in the grass in the northwest corner [of the Plaza.] Funds to pay for it were donated by the dog's many friends," the same paper wrote.

The plaque reads:

In Memory of Our Community Dog
Mike
Self-appointed guardian of the Plaza, official welcomer of visitors and general ambassador of good will, Ol' Mike was known and beloved by all.
Regardless of race, color, creed, or station in life, he was a silent, tolerant, loyal friend.
Early 1945 to December 14, 1960
Take heed if you will: a moral lies within.

AS TIME WENT ON, Prescott's Plaza grew rich in history, hosting both annual and special events. In 1909, President Taft spoke there. It also saw the launching of Barry Goldwater's and John McCain's Republican presidential campaigns. The Plaza has been and will undoubtedly remain a beloved Prescott attraction for the foreseeable future.

15

ARIZONA'S FIRST MASONS STEERED EARLY PRESCOTT

By Drew Desmond

It is difficult today to understand the social gravity and importance of fraternal organizations in the nineteenth century. These were the places where "networking" occurred. Generally, each fraternal organization represented a particular group of socioeconomic class or trade and instilled a sense of duty and civic improvement. The Masons were the business owners, lawyers, doctors and politicians. Indeed, organizing Arizona's first Masonic lodge in Prescott was considered so important that one was established even before the appearance of a denominational church.

Less than a year after Prescott was founded, in June 1865, the dispensation for the charter of a Masonic lodge was granted by California. The application, penned by master of the lodge John T. Alsip, stated, "This is a small community, far removed from others—an advanced post in the army of civilization—fighting against barbarism, with a hostile and savage foe around and depending only upon our own armed hands for the safety of life and property. But I say proudly, nowhere are the Constitutions of Masonry more cherished and loved or its principles better or nobly illustrated."

The lodge was called Aztlan Lodge, No. 1, Free and Accepted Masons. The first three meetings of the lodge were held in the governor's house. In addition to the usual Masonic exercises, it was explained at these meetings that the needs of the infant town and how these men of power

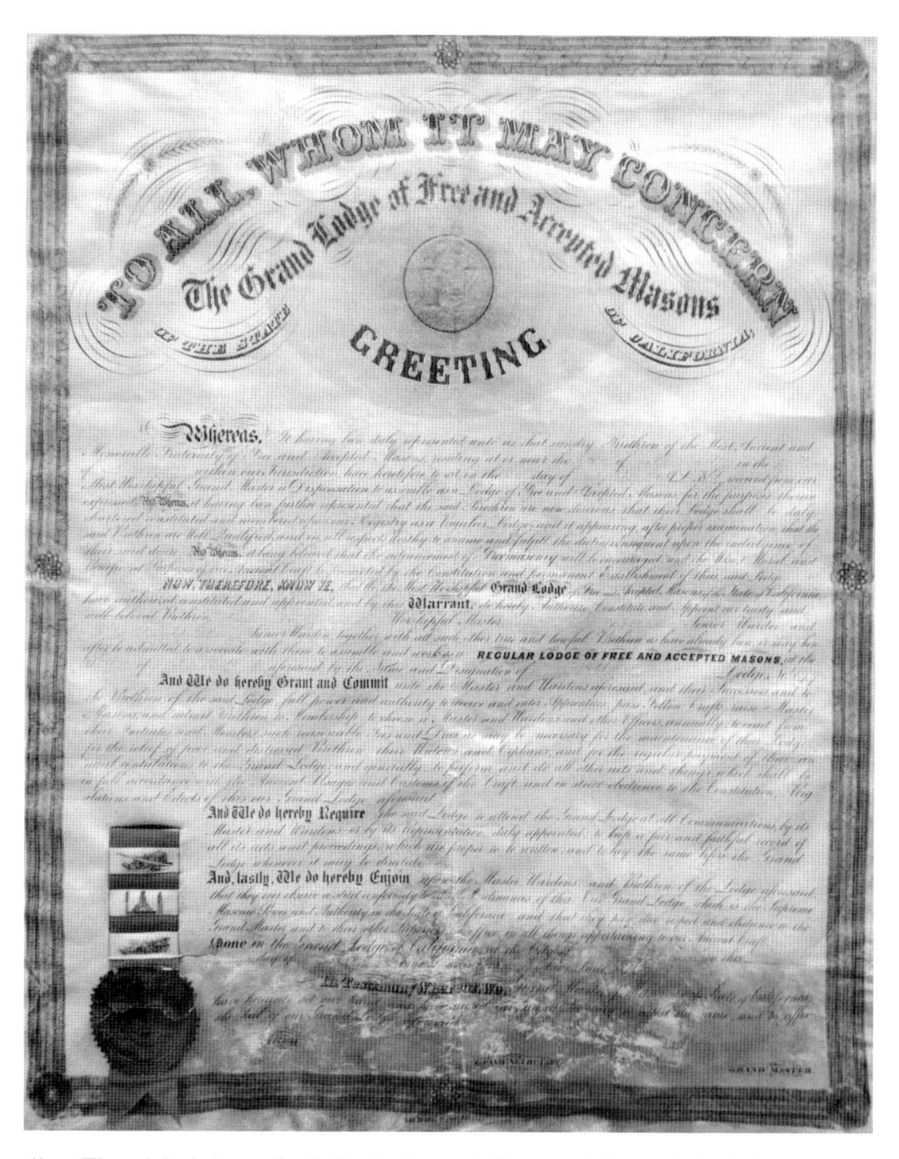

TO ALL WHOM IT MAY CONCERN

The Grand Lodge of Free and Accepted Masons

OF THE STATE OF CALIFORNIA

GREETING

Whereas,

NOW, THEREFORE, KNOW YE, Grand Lodge Warrant

REGULAR LODGE OF FREE AND ACCEPTED MASONS

And We do hereby Grant and Commit

And We do hereby Require

And, lastly, We do hereby Enjoin

Done in the Grand Lodge of California

GRAND MASTER

Above: The original charter for Aztlan Lodge no. 1, Prescott, Arizona. *Aztlan Lodge no. 1.*

Opposite: The original cornerstone of the building. *Aztlan Lodge no. 1.*

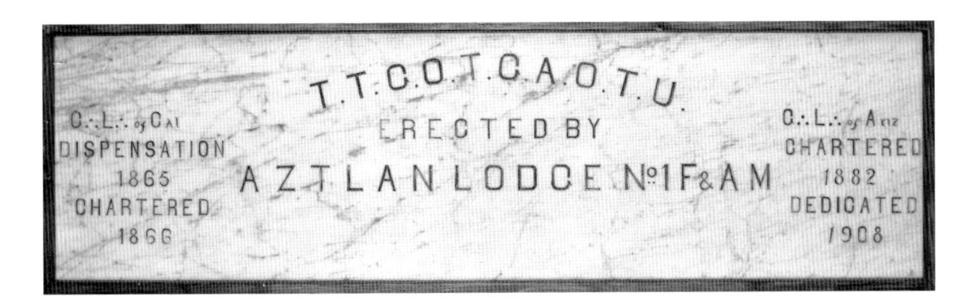

and capital could see them achieved were discussed. For a time, meeting locations were either rented or shared. In 1902, a fifty-foot-wide lot was purchased for $5,000, and six years later, the iconic lodge building on Cortez Street was completed.

"A California builder won the $38,042 construction contract, [and] the temple was dedicated, with due pomp and circumstance, [on] November 17, 1908," Morris Goldwater once wrote. The Masons occupied the upper floors of the building while renting the street-level spaces to businesses, doctors and attorneys. It would not be surprising to discover that several of these tenants were fellow Masons.

Eventually, one Mason rose high above the others: Morris Goldwater. No one had a larger influence on the development of Prescott than Goldwater. In 1964, he was named "Prescott's Man of the Century." Goldwater was also awarded the extraordinary, rare and highest Masonic honor of the thirty-third degree, which is reserved for men with the stature of George Washington.

A case containing all of Morris Goldwater's Masonic effects still resides in the Masons' current location on Willow Creek Road. The case's plaque reads: "This case containing the Masonic effects of Morris Goldwater, 33rd degree, was presented to Aztlan Lodge #1 by Barry Morris Goldwater, 32nd degree, in recognition of the place this lodge held in the heart of his uncle." Thirty-second-degree Barry was, of course, a longtime U.S. senator and Republican presidential candidate in 1964. Included inside this case is a potential treasure trove of historic information in the form of a large stack of yellowed correspondences, which Morris, the lodge's historian, deemed important enough to preserve.

In the early 1980s, the temple on Cortez Street was added to the National Register of Historic Places. Needing a more modern location with an elevator, the Masons then sold the building to Prescott Historic Properties for $212,000, and the organization soon embarked on an ambitious six-and-a-half-year-long restoration.

Today's lodge hall is a typical Masonic representation of Solomon's Temple. However, the chairs and pillars are the original items that came around the horn, landed in San Francisco and were carried over land by freighters.

Like other fraternal organizations, the Masons were a secret society, and those early conversations about how to steer Prescott are forever lost to history.

16

PRESCOTT AND AUTOMOBILES

Love at First Sight

BY DREW DESMOND

The first automobile to drive into Prescott was also the first type of car to ever be mass produced: a brand-new 1903 "Curved Dash" Oldsmobile. It was the evening of February 26, 1903, and the welcoming of this new invention brought a surprising amount of civic pride to the city. "Prescott is fast becoming a metropolitan city," the *Courier* proclaimed. "A brand-new automobile was seen last night on the street."

The car belonged to champion shooter, avid hunter and popular Jerome merchant, Walter C. Miller, who made the trip with his associate L.A. Hawkins. The automobile journey did not start in Jerome, however.

Back then, roads were simply wide, well-used, horse trails. They were littered with rocks, roots, holes and occasional mud holes and washouts. Even worse, what is known today as Highway 89A did not exist. The only way from Jerome to Prescott was a circuitous, rough trip through the towns of Cottonwood, Cherry and Dewey. So, instead of taking the car the entire way, Miller took his Oldsmobile on the train to travel from Jerome-to-Jerome Junction, located just south of Chino Valley on the Prescott–Ash Fork line. Today, the location of this former rail connection is located within Chino's town limits.

The two men reported it was "a rather hard trip, as much sand was encountered, which does not add in the least to the joy of the automobilist," the *Courier* pointed out. The seventeen-mile trip from the junction to Prescott took them a bone-shaking hour and a half to complete.

Technically, Miller's Oldsmobile was not the first automobile ever seen in Prescott. "There was a machine here with a circus, but that one was such a poor specimen that Mr. Miller can well be awarded the palm for bringing the first automobile that really would 'auto' to Prescott," the *Courier* related.

The two men spent only one night in Prescott before returning to Jerome. "Even though their stay was short, the gentlemen and their carriage are very welcome to come back again and stay longer," the same paper wrote.

Despite the widespread civic pride, not everyone was impressed. When Miller brought his Oldsmobile into the Plaza Stables, where it spent the night, the man in charge drolly asked, "Shall I give him oats and groom him?"

"It will not be long," the *Courier* predicted, "until many autos will glide along our streets, making the onward march of progress and the growth of Prescott to a large city." Indeed, these machines, as they were often called, would begin to infiltrate every aspect of life in Prescott.

In late April 1903, "an automobile party arrived in town, and the machines…attracted a great deal of interest from the residents of this little mountain city, where automobiles are as scarce as honest politicians," the *Miner* declared. The party was attempting to drive from Tucson to the Grand Canyon. However, the Old Black Canyon stage road was in no condition to accommodate automobile traffic. One machine broke down and "had to be hauled into Mayer on a freight wagon." While the party waited for parts to arrive from back east, they completed their journey to the canyon via the railroad. Upon their return, they drove from Mayer into Prescott, causing the spectacle.

It was an individual from this same party who gave the editor of the *Miner* his first ride in an automobile: "The trip extended beyond Whipple," the editor conveyed, "and you '*auto*' have seen that auto skim along over the smooth road. The machine is capable of making 35 mph, and as the road north of town is nice and smooth, [the driver] let the thing out, just to give the scribe a sensation of high life for a few brief moments."

Around this time, Joseph Mayer, the founder of the town that was named after him, experienced his first ride in an automobile. The roads there must have been in a worse condition, as he described his experience as "just like riding in a wheelbarrow," but he said he still envisioned that "after a while, there wouldn't be any more horses."

Some immediately thought of the potential entrepreneurial uses these machines could provide, like what might be called Prescott's first taxicab: "Ira Pulliam's automobile arrived yesterday and will be put into commission at once for the carrying of passengers and picnic parties. He will undoubtedly do a big business with the machine, as the automobile fever has struck this city pretty hard," the *Miner* chronicled. Pulliam's car could carry up to four passengers.

In order to "drive" more business to his new hotel (which still stands today), A.J. Head was the first to offer free automobile transit to his modern lodging.

Not everyone thought highly of the new invention, however. Frank Murphy, who brought the railroad to Prescott, disliked the automobile. He forbade them from entering the property he controlled in west Prescott "until such time as the horses have become more accustomed to the machines and not because Mr. Murphy is not in sympathy with the introduction of up-to-date methods in our community," the *Miner* reported. Although he would eventually allow cars on the western streets, Murphy never allowed them on Murphy Drive, which crossed through the park of the same name.

Early automobiles were often in need of repair, and early mechanics grew out of machine shops. The first machine shop in Prescott to advertise a specialty in auto repair belonged to W.T. Hall.

In 1903, dealerships were known as "agencies." In July, "Samuel Hill Hardware company took the agency for the famous Oldsmobile automobiles....On account of the tremendous demand for the machines in the East, the company has been unable to fill the entire order, but shipped two machines which were already sold," the *Miner* reported. Later, the Sam Hill store would become the agency for Ford. In November, the Bashford-Burmister Company became the agency for Cadillac and kept one of them for business use. "It is one of the handsomest autos yet received in this part of the country."

Automobiles immediately made their way into the holidays. Fourth of July 1903 saw the first automobile in a Prescott parade. "It will take the place of Bill Dugan's calliope of last year," the *Miner* said, "but will not make nearly as much noise."

The first year with the horseless carriage in Prescott ended appropriately with this visage in a downtown store window: "The RH Burmister & Sons company have an original and very unique window display," the *Miner* reported. "It is a representation of Santa Claus driving through a representation of snow in an automobile loaded with all sorts of Christmas goods."

Mere months after the automobile's first entrance, everyone knew it was here to stay.

THE PHOENIX GAZETTE CUP

By 1910, there were several manufacturers of cars, and debates about which was best were lively. Soon, the autos were put to the test in a race from Prescott to Phoenix. Specifically, the finish line was located on West Adams Street in front of the *Arizona Gazette*'s office, who sponsored the trophy.

Nineteen cars would attempt to win the premier event. When it was all over, only one was able to drive back to Prescott.

The race started in front of the Prescott National Bank on Cortez Street. The crowd that appeared was quite large, considering the 6:30 a.m. start. The trip was to follow the old stage route: from Prescott to Mayer, Humboldt, Cordes, Black Canyon, Goddard, New River and, finally, to Phoenix, ending at the newspaper office.

The rules were fairly simple. Participants had to be Yavapai County residents. Each car had to run the entire race under its own power. Also, "when any car in the race approaches within one hundred feet of the one ahead and desires to pass and signals this desire by two honks, the car in front must turn to the right, giving half the road and allow it to pass; the passing car must pass to the left," the *Miner* outlined.

The nineteen entrants were driving ten different models of cars: five raced Buicks, three drove Fords, two drove Cadillacs and two drove Tourists. And there was one car each representing: Overland, Premier, Regal, Reo, Stearns and Stoddard-Dayton. Due to the variety of horsepower in the cars' engines, those with less power were given carefully thought-out handicaps. Each auto would start, one at a time, at five-minute intervals.

All of the automobiles had at least one passenger. A foresighted few brought along a "mechanician." Despite the known dangers, one man brought along his family of five.

The most charming entrant was the one and only female driver, Mrs. H.T. Southworth, who was behind the wheel of her two-year-old, twenty-horsepower Ford.

T.G. Norris, in his Tourist, and H.D. Aitken, manning his Cadillac, had a side bet; the loser had to provide a banquet for all the people who made the trip. Norris was to start before Aitken and suggested that once he got started, he "never expect[ed] to see him again until the celebration of the festivities." For Aitken's part, he said that "he will not take any mud from his…competitor."

When the race commenced, the only thing faster than the cars were the mounting mechanical malfunctions. The Imperial was the first casualty.

Hitting an extreme road hazard, the driver "broke a knuckle on the wheel, [and] his escape from serious injury was considered marvelous," the *Miner* proclaimed. The next to have trouble was the Reo. It "went out of commission due to some mechanical derangement." But after a delay lasting to 3:00 p.m., it was "on the road again, passing Humboldt at a rapid clip." Norris, the side-better in his Tourist, had trouble with his steering but was able to make the repair relatively quickly and charged on. The Stearns auto was a favorite to win the race and was doing well, but near Blue Bell Siding, it struck a rut in the road and broke its axle. One of the Cadillacs had a "narrow escape from a tragic fate" when it struck a large pothole at the Arizona Canal and lost its removable cabin roof. The women in the car were violently thrown into the air but fortunately landed back inside the vehicle. After finishing the race, the passengers of that Cadillac went back to retrieve the lost wreckage. One of the Buicks had the most annoying time, suffering no less than seventeen tire punctures along the way.

Although the roads were thought to be in fairly good condition going into the race, the exact opposite was true. "From [Cordes] to Phoenix, all semblance of a road had passed into a myth, and after the many cars had passed over it, the mechanical autopsy held in Phoenix was the best evidence that it had seen better days," the *Miner* observed. As of noon the next day, three cars had not arrived in Phoenix, and "several relief parties [had] been sent out to hunt for the derelicts."

The matter of the side bet between Norris and Aitkens turned frightful for a time, as Aitkens had not shown up in Phoenix. His panicked employer, the Bashford-Burmister Company, asked that "no expense be spared" to locate the company's secretary. It took Aitken over twenty-four hours to reach Phoenix. He said "that the greater part of Sunday night was passed using the cushion as a headrest, which was the only soothing balm of this memorial trip." Losing the bet, Aitken was supposed to pay for a banquet for the drivers and passengers of the race—a total of sixty-five people. However, Norris magnanimously paid for half.

All the cars, except for the Stoddard-Dayton, "passed through a series of distressing accidents," and except for this one car, all the rest would be "sent back by train."

Despite one car suffering seventeen flats, all five of the Buicks finished, as did two out of three of the Fords. The only other car that was able to complete the race was the Tourist.

Al Weber broke the all-time record for the trip (five hours, forty minutes) in his forty-horsepower Buick and would have won the trophy, except he left three minutes after his starting time. Instead, the only lady driver in the race, Mrs. H.T. Southworth, won the Arizona Gazette Cup. Although she was given a fifty-five-minute handicap, she still made the 110-mile trip in a remarkable six hours and thirty-three minutes. After her handicap was applied, she won the race by one minute. Who said women take longer than men to get ready?

Early Traffic Laws

The teen years of the twentieth century brought an awkward adolescence when it came to street traffic, and a flurry of primitive traffic ordinances became necessary. Animals and autos did not mix well on the same path. Car clubs suggested rules that were eventually adopted nationwide. Yet when it came to issues specific to individual towns, some of these primitive traffic laws are sure to bring a smile to today's reader.

In Prescott, the major issue was the interaction of mechanical automobiles and beasts of burden (mostly horses and mules). Traffic was becoming crowded and dangerous for everyone. As far as Prescott was concerned, it was thought animals should take priority.

In March 1915, several editions of the *Miner* published a letter from Robert Robbins, the chief of police, demanding compliance of the newly adopted "Ordinance No. 208, regulating street traffic." The situation must have become acute, as Robbins had been "instructed by the Common [City] Council to rigidly enforce [its] provisions." This letter was a strict warning to motorists. The town fathers were fed up.

Some of the provisions adopted seem quite commonsensical to us today, but when motorized traffic was in its infancy, the most basic things needed to be pointed out. "All persons driving or operating a motor vehicle on the streets must keep to the right of the center of such street," the letter read, "and upon overcoming or passing any other vehicle, must pass to the left." Motorists were also told to imagine the very center point of an intersection; if making a right turn, one must not pass that center point. When one making a left turn, they must pass that center point before turning. The ordinance continues: "All motor vehicles shall have a signaling device [and] must display at least one white light in front and one red in the rear when traveling at night." The only requirement to be a legal driver then was to be eighteen years old. Those younger could also drive but not without "a written permit from the clerk of the common council."

In the early days of automobiles, speed was not always measured in miles per hour. In Prescott, there was to be "a speed limit of one mile in four minutes [fifteen miles per hour] in the business section [and] one mile in three minutes [twenty miles per hour] elsewhere in the city limits."

Aside from the most basic of road rules, Ordinance No. 208 would safeguard street animals at all costs: "A driver of a motor vehicle must use all precautions to ensure [the] safety of persons on foot and to prevent frightening animals which are being ridden, driven or led," the *Miner* reported. "A driver must stop a motor vehicle at request of a person riding, leading, or driving a restive animal and, if necessary, must also stop [the] motor."

Outlawing impairments to driving was not even a consideration then.

17

SMOKING MARIJUANA WAS A COMMUNITY EVENT

By Drew Desmond

In the 1910s, marijuana was not only legal, but in Prescott, it was immensely popular. Many organizations held what was called "smoker" events, where groups numbering three figures would gather to get high. The largest smoker events were annually hosted by the Yavapai Chamber of Commerce. In reporting on the 1916 Chamber Smoker on February 16, the *Miner* was undoubtedly responsible for one of the first printed uses of the word "weed" in reference to marijuana:

PLAN BIG TIME AT
CHAMBER SMOKER
SHORT SNAPPY SPEECHES,
PLENTY OF THE WEED,
LIGHT LUNCH & MUSIC ON PROGRAM

Tickets cost about seventy-five cents (around the price of an expensive restaurant dinner today), and to justify the price, it was noted that the gate charge would just cover the cost of the entertainment.

Smoker events were always advertised as informal affairs that included music and various speakers. "The principal reason for the holding of this 'smokefest,'" the *Miner* explained, was "to create a feeling of good fellowship among the members" of the chamber and its associates. Historically, it has been rumored that smoking marijuana might accomplish just that. Smokers were optimistic gatherings, spreading hope for a prosperous year. At the 1916 Chamber Smoker, "Mr. Hard Times" was killed and buried with a full funeral service.

The first recorded smoker event occurred in September 1909, as the National Guard of Arizona was "extended lavish and hearty hospitality… in a manner that will be long remembered by its recipients," the *Miner* reported. Officers went to the Yavapai Club for a lavish banquet, while noncommissioned officers and privates were, at the same time, at the Elks Theater, enjoying a smoker. "Unbounded enthusiasm prevailed" at the Elks, "where patriotism ran riot." In the early part of the evening, the soldiers played cards while imbibing, and around 11:00 p.m., Governor Sloan and Colonel McClintock arrived from the Yavapai Club. After some "stirring speeches," food was served, "and after that, there ensued a scene never before witnessed in Prescott.

"The band started playing Sousa's 'Double Eagle March.'" The men paired up, including the governor and the colonel, "and a grand march was begun," the *Miner* said. Even the citizen spectators were swept up in the spirit and joined the parade, when "pandemonium broke loose, and for twenty minutes, the theater shook with such yelling and cheering as is seldom witnessed outside of big political conventions." The playing of "Dixie" and the "Star-Spangled Banner" repeated the demonstrations. "Refreshments were again served and after a social period the gathering dispersed at midnight."

In November 1909, astronomer Percival Lowell, the founder of the Lowell Observatory in Flagstaff, where Pluto was later discovered, came south to Prescott to, in part, get high. A renowned scientist in his own time, Lowell came to Prescott over the Thanksgiving holiday of 1909 to spend time with his friend Judge E.M. Doe.

Lowell would also take this opportunity to give a spellbinding lecture to a delighted crowd at the Elks' Theater about the potential of intelligent life on Mars. "It was Prof. Lowell who first offered proof to show that Mars is inhabited," the *Miner* proclaimed, "and because of his achievements has been honored with membership by the highest scientific societies of Europe." Although it's not widely publicized at the Lowell Observatory today, Percival, "a millionaire several times," originally built his observatory in the hopes of spying a civilization on Mars. Indeed, that was the reason for naming the observatory's perch Mars Hill. The less-powerful telescopes of the day seemed to show straight-lined canals on the surface of Mars, and Lowell wanted a more powerful telescope to take a closer look. He built the modern observatory at his own expense. He chose Flagstaff for its high elevation, often clear skies and remoteness from city lights. This was the first time anyone had taken these factors into consideration when placing a telescope, and it is something that has been practiced ever since.

His speech at the Elk's Theater made a lasting impression. The "lecture on astronomical subjects was a treat such as has never before been enjoyed in the city," the *Miner* crowed.

After the lecture, the Yavapai Club held a smoker event to honor both Professor Lowell and the new commanding officer at Whipple Barracks, Major Kirby. "Good fellowship, excellent speeches and a general fine time were the features of the smoker tendered last evening," the same paper declared. It "was one of the most pleasing affairs that has ever been given at the Yavapai Club, which is famed for its hospitality." The smoker was attended "by nearly one hundred members of the club, and the merrymaking continued until the clock struck 12." It is likely that Lowell's host, Judge Doe, as well as many other local dignitaries, were in attendance.

The military members at Whipple, particularly the officers, were often invited to smokers. Additionally, several smokers were held specifically to offer some rest and recreation for the troops. The Prescott National Guard, Company E, held a smoker in March 1910, which, according to the *Miner*, was attended by "nearly one hundred prominent business and professional men." These men included former attorney general E.S. Clark, Mayor Morris Goldwater and several judges. The "purpose of the gathering… was to stir up enthusiasm for the company and to secure the active support (moral and financial) of the community." After the "refreshments," eight men spoke about some of the history of the national guard and its worthiness of support. "The smoker soon afterward broke up, with appreciation of a pleasant evening," the paper said.

On July 15, 1911, officers from Camp Brodie were entertained at a smoker in the assembly hall of the Yavapai Club. Several prominent Prescott citizens performed skits or musical numbers. "Col. Tuthill, on behalf of the officers, stated that the encampment had been most enjoyable and the officers as well as the men were exceedingly grateful to the people of Prescott for the hospitable manner in which they had been entertained," the *Miner* related.

Occasionally, smokers were held for the purpose of networking among civic organizations. "The bankers and good roads advocates all united in an informal social gathering…at the Yavapai Club; the affair being termed a 'smoker,'" the *Miner* reported. An orchestra played, and several theater people offered entertainment. "There were two toastmasters or ringmasters, as they were humorously termed, for the speech making. Morris Goldwater represented the bankers, while T.G. Norris officiated on behalf of the Good Roads Association." The fun continued until midnight, when Mayor Goldwater announced that it was his bedtime on that Tuesday night, "and the genial company then dispersed. The visitors particularly sounded the praise of Prescott and her lavish and hearty hospitality."

In 1916, a smoker was hosted by the Yavapai Cattlemen's Association for the area's cowboys and ranchers. "They were entertained, with all conceivable entertainment ending in the 'smoker,' which was, beyond doubt, the crowning feature of one round of grand hospitality," the *Miner* declared.

Although marijuana was legal, social stigma forbade women from smoking anything in public. As a result, some smoker events devolved into elements one would expect to see at a stag party. Such was the case at the annual Chamber of Commerce Smoker in 1917. The chamber chairman promised that it "will appeal to each and every citizen of Yavapai County, as well as those from the outside," the *Miner* claimed. "It is the opinion of the reception and entertainment committee that a smoker, attended by every citizen of the county at which short snappy speeches will be made, will tend not only to be a source of entertainment to the members and their guests but will instill a greater interest in the workings of the organizations."

"It Looks Like a Big Night Tonight" the headline crowed. "Promptly at 8:30...the fireworks will commence, and from that time on, there will not be one dull moment in the entire program." Advance ticket sales already guaranteed that this smoker would be "the largest crowd in the history of the chamber....The chief function of the affair will be entertainment, musical and otherwise." The Prescott Band would provide the music. After the affair, the *Miner* revealed:

> *Truly the most unique stunt ever staged by a civic organization in the history of the world was pulled off at the annual smoker of the Yavapai Chamber of Commerce. Space will not permit a full account of the arrival of Miss Prosperity...* [but] *the ovation which was accorded* [her] *on her natal day will mark an epoch in the history of the Yavapai Chamber of Commerce....The whoops and yells resounded from Thumb Butte to Fort Whipple.*

Evidently, Miss Prosperity was a pretty young thing.

Many fraternal organizations held smokers as well. In March 1917, "the local Yavapai Council of the Knights of Columbus entertained AG Bagley, special supreme agent," for a smoker at the Council Hall. "Some twenty-five members of the local council were in attendance at the smoker," the *Miner* reported.

"Successful in every particular was the smoker given by the Odd Fellows lodge of this city" the following month. It featured music and messages from Judge Frank O. Smith and Reverend Joel Hedgpeth. "During the intermissions in the program, the smokers smoked, played cards and amused themselves generally."

In 1924, a smoker was held in conjunction with the Arizona Good Roads Convention and included four other Yavapai civic boards and organizations. In total, 150 people took part, and the *Miner* recounted the atmosphere:

> *In point of enthusiasm, the smoker-banquet resembled a national convention…the delegates coming from all parts of Arizona…for a dinner and a smoker that was an exceedingly lively and peppy affair. During the dinner, the quartet…kept the ball rolling with catchy and clever songs and parodies. The delegates became so enthusiastic as a result that they caught the spirit of the entertainers joining in the merriment with a riot of music, song and badinage* [humorous or witty conversation].

The popularity of smokers began to decline, however, and soon, marijuana was made illegal and stigmatized for nearly a century. However, in 2020, Arizona voters passed an initiative making the recreational use of marijuana legal again by a margin of 60 to 40 percent.

18

PRESCOTT'S FIRST MOTORCYCLE CLUB

By Drew Desmond

In 1911, motorcycles were closer to what people might call motorbikes today. Early machines had pedals like a bicycle. Single-cylinder engines produced a meager four horsepower, while two-cycle engines produced seven horsepower. Still, like the automobile, motorcycling proved popular, and on March 10, 1911, several enthusiasts formed the Yavapai Motorcycle Club.

Ray Vyne was the club's first president. The club was "intended to institute club runs, hill climbing contests, etc., and trophies will be hung up for such events," the *Miner* explained.

The club's first project was to institute racing events for the upcoming 1911 Frontier Days in July. The fair had already introduced automobile racing, and the addition of motorcycle contests brought these portions of Frontier Days the moniker of "gasoline events." The track that was used was the old horse racing track, and its condition was poor. "Deep furrows and gulches served to make fast driving on the stretches impossible, and all of the turns were inches deep in sand," the *Miner* reported.

There was also a five-mile-long race for bikes with twin-cylinder engines, even though only two such bikes existed in town. Both were manufactured by "Indian" and despite the lack of competition, spectators were thrilled by a close race.

Both sized engines ran together in the other three events. There was a three-mile-long "Handicap Free-For-All," in which the bikes with smaller engines got a one-eighth-of-a-mile head start. It turned out to be not nearly enough.

The first ever running of an "Australian Pursuit Race" in Yavapai County featured bikes spread out on the track one-eighth of a mile apart. If a bike was passed, it was eliminated, and this continued until only one rider remained. It took two and a half miles of running before one of the Indians won the novel contest.

The remaining two motorcycle events were a bit odd. The engines were turned off for the "Emergency Race." This race was inspired by those times when one's engine failed. It was a one-hundred-yard-long pedaling race. One rider, desperate to gain the early lead, had his hopes dashed when, at the start, he exerted his full force on the pedal and broke it clean off.

Perhaps the most unconventional event was the "Slow Race." The object of this contest was to finish last. "This unusual contest was more a trial of patience than of skill," the *Miner* noted. Six riders entered. They could not touch their feet to the ground, and "slipping clutches and loose belts were barred." At the start, "two of the riders added a touch of humor to the situation by [immediately] falling off their machines. Doris of Phoenix succeeded in coming in last and defeating Belding, who was making every effort to stand still without showing any signs of hesitation," the paper joked.

In 1913, these races were extended to a new, much longer course. "The Prescott Loop" was used for racing both motorcycles and automobiles and became renowned across the state. Racers began at ten-minute intervals "to insure a continuous thrill," the *Miner* observed. Shortly after the last bike started, the first bikes began returning.

The start was located at the Courthouse Plaza. The course then ran east on Gurley Street to Mt. Vernon Street, where it turned north to the Jerome Junction Road and then returned via the American Ranch. It then reentered Prescott "by way of Mercy Hospital at Grove Avenue and [turned] onto Gurley Street and thence proceed[ed] down Gurley to Mt. Vernon once more," the *Miner* explained. The finish line was located at the Plaza.

For safety, Gurley Street in the downtown district was roped off, and a watch kept at Miller Valley. As soon as a racer passed that point, word was telephoned into Prescott, and warning was given through an alarm from the fire bell. "This will ensure that the streets will be clear so that the machine can go down on its way at full speed," the paper explained. Mastering the curves at the intersections of Gurley Street at Grove Street and Gurley Street at Mt. Vernon Street was considered particularly challenging.

The Yavapai Motorcycle Club was the perfect host to visiting competitors. A "splendid impression [was] made on Phoenix motorcyclists by the spread at the Yavapai Motorcycle Club on the occasion of the July 4 visit at Prescott," the *Arizona Republican* stated. "The cozy club rooms, the magnificent banquet right in the club [and] the feeling of perfect accord among the members could not have failed to make an impression on the chugbike adventurers."

In September 1913, the motorcycle club took it upon itself to install crossroad signs around the Prescott Loop. "The signs [had] an orange background with black letters symbolic of the club's colors," the *Miner* noted. The signs bore "inscriptions pointing to the various roads which must be taken in order to reach certain points. In addition, the distances from the crossroads to the various towns in the county [were] stated."

The following year, during the 1914 Frontier Days, the endurance of these machines was tested to the limit. A course was set to start in Phoenix at the board of trade and travel to Prescott, with one lap around the forty-three-mile-long Prescott Loop before finishing at the Plaza. In order to finish in a timely fashion in Prescott, riders started in Phoenix at 5:30 in the morning. The boys from Maricopa County won all of the $250 purse, but it was hardly a windfall. When they calculated their expenses for participating, they totaled $256.

19

TRUE TALES OF PROHIBITION

By Drew Desmond

Prohibition of alcohol was never popular in Yavapai County. Many times, the Yavapai County sheriff declined to make arrests. Other times, those who were charged were let go by sympathetic juries. However, this was not the case for "Dutch" John Berrent.

When Prohibition was set to start, John had the entrepreneurial idea to stock up an inventory of alcohol the size of a distributor. He later admitted to a court that he had bought "twenty-five gallons of whiskey and fifty cases of beer…for his own use" during Prohibition, but he was known to spread the joy.

Soon, the sheriff's office would also become aware of Dutch John's notoriety. After selling three bottles to one paid informant and two bottles to J.W. Rieff of the Thiele Detective Agency of Los Angeles, Dutch John found himself before a court judge. Across from him lay "273 bottles of beer; [along with] 23 pints, 2 quarts and 3 five-gallon [glass jugs] of whiskey," which was found inside his premises, according to the *Miner*.

Every witness the state brought in testified they had bought alcohol from him, but Dutch John flatly denied this. When Rieff's two pints were entered into evidence, it was noticed that they were less than halfway full. The courtroom erupted into laughter when the private detective insisted that he had to have a taste to make sure it was really whiskey.

When the proceedings were finished, Dutch John was found guilty. However, before he was sentenced, he sued the justice of the peace to have the bulk of the spiritous liquids returned to him, as he was never accused of selling more than the five pints. Due to a loophole in the prohibition law, Dutch John was given his booze back.

This caused consternation for the sentencing judge, who told Dutch John that he would give him a lighter sentence if he would both confess to the crime and allow the county authorities to destroy the rest of his stock. Wanting his hooch returned, John refused and spent the next eight months in jail; he also paid a $300 fine. It was the stiffest sentence any bootlegger had ever received in Yavapai County.

Predictably, the harsh sentence was not enough to set Dutch John onto the straight and narrow. After only four months out of jail, he was again arrested for bootlegging.

Dutch John had taken a rail trip to Albuquerque, New Mexico, under the watchful eye of a Wells Fargo detective. On his return, it was noticed that he had acquired four mysterious barrels marked "Household Goods," "Glassware," "This End Up," and "Handle Carefully." Eventually, these four barrels were connected to John, and when they were opened, it was found that each contained a ten-gallon keg of whiskey.

The court was less than merciful toward Dutch John, sending him to jail after he was unable to pay a hefty $750 bail. Later, the bail was increased to $1,000, an amount unheard of at the time for a bootlegging case.

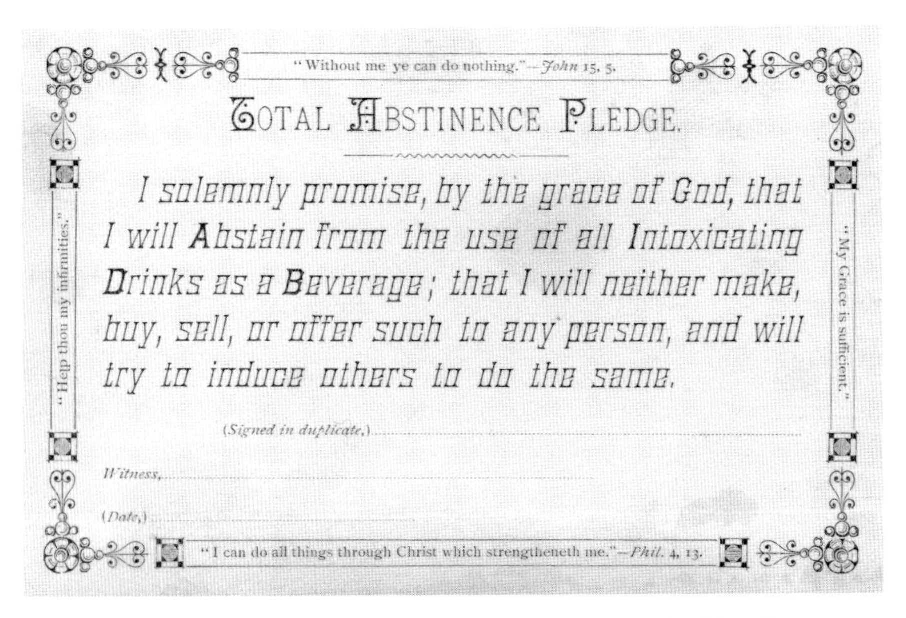

"Without me ye can do nothing."—*John* 15. 5.

TOTAL ABSTINENCE PLEDGE.

I solemnly promise, by the grace of God, that I will Abstain from the use of all Intoxicating Drinks as a Beverage; that I will neither make, buy, sell, or offer such to any person, and will try to induce others to do the same.

(*Signed in duplicate*,) ....

Witness, ...

(*Date*,) ....

"Help thou my infirmities."

"My Grace is sufficient."

"I can do all things through Christ which strengtheneth me."—*Phil.* 4, 13.

Prior to and during Prohibition, signing abstinence pledges was popular. *Nancy Burgess.*

Dutch John must have realized that he would be facing a heavy sentence and that Arizona authorities would always keep an eye on him, so he started to formulate an escape.

John was a good prisoner and "considered harmless." As a result, he was allowed out of his cell to do some odd jobs to "supplement his slender resources and aid his digestion," the *Miner* disclosed. So, at 10:00 a.m. on Easter Sunday, when the streets were empty and the churches were full, Dutch John quietly slipped out the jail's western door.

"The sheriff's office is confident that the old fellow will be seen and apprehended again," the *Miner* reported. "His portion is likely to be an unpalatable one if he allows himself to come once more within the clutches of the law. If he is hiding, his cover is a good one; if he is making tracks out of the purview of the authorities here, his tracks are well concealed; he must only travel by night."

Dutch John had devised the perfect escape. Neither hide nor hair was ever seen of him again in Arizona. It is assumed that he drifted to moister climates.

Countywide, it was not long before any libations bought before Prohibition ran out. Although it is probable that stills were put to work almost immediately, law enforcement did not seize many for the first four years of Prohibition. Then, starting in 1919, a crackdown on the illegal practice revealed just how wily and creative many of the bootleggers had become.

According to the book *Ranch Trails and Short Tales* by Claire Champie Cordes, Fred Cordes had what must have been a typical set-up in Yavapai County. She wrote:

> *During Prohibition, we decided we should have a little whiskey on hand in case of snake bite or something, so Fred began to fashion a still from my old copper washing boiler. He soldered a valve on the lid, got some copper pipe from an old mill, coiled it into circles and started looking for a place to hide it. There was an old mining tunnel a couple hundred yards down the creek below our place. Tall bushes grew in front of the tunnel, so he figured it was the right place. The next time he got barley for the horses, he ordered a hundred pounds of oats or rye. In an old wooden barrel, he built a fire to make a nice clean char. He put rye, sugar and water in the barrel to ferment.*

Cordes's hooch was double filtered through crushed charcoal and then sand. "The results proved to be very satisfying," she wrote. "One friend, a neighbor of ours, insisted he needed some for his sick wife. We sold him a quart for five dollars, a lot of money in those days."

Indeed, hiding one's still was vital. It could be argued that the best hiding places were never found and are therefore lost to history. However, some of the discovered still operations impressed both the newspapers and law enforcement. One outfit, described by the *Miner* as "the most elaborate discovered for years was unearthed in a raid in the Verde District." It could have doubled as a man cave. It "was excavated at a distance of twenty feet from a well, its roof being about four feet below the surface of the ground. The room was ten square feet with walls six feet high and could be reached only by a tunnel running from the well with the opening twelve feet below the well curb," the paper reported. The smokestack was cleverly run through a horseshoe forge from which one might expect to see smoke—but not constantly. This was its downfall.

Another bootlegger, Frank Leonard, constructed a complete shop. "Their little place, located up in Government Canyon, was just close enough to the city to make it convenient to market the product, yet it was secluded enough to be safe," the *Miner* revealed. Leonard's production house had a cement floor, drainage and full ventilation. The paper described it as "most comfortable as well as private. In it, he had installed substantial kettles, boilers, vats, mixing vessels and a good-sized copper still."

When the sheriff arrived to arrest Leonard, his wife refused to go without a fight. She "bit, scratched and squawked" and then drew a pistol, the *Miner* detailed. While she was being disarmed, Mr. Leonard, now handcuffed, tried to make his escape but stopped when warned that the officer would shoot.

A far more serious skirmish occurred outside of Dewey in 1920. It resulted in Deputy Sheriff T.J. Marks being shot in the arm as he and other officers closed in on the residence of Charles G. Bly. After eluding police for two weeks, Bly was finally caught and served several months for moonshining. However, he beat the charge of assault by arguing that he did not know who was approaching his place and reacted to protect his life and property. Deputy Marks required at least one operation, and it took months for his arm to heal.

"Illicit stills, grading all the way from a small gas stove with a can and a copper pipe to the modern and fully equipped article have been raided and confiscated," the *Miner* reported. One man "seized upon the idea of making fire water out of a fire-preventer" when he fashioned a still out of a fire extinguisher. "With a few lengths of tubing and a little solder, he had arranged the proper outlets for the steam," the same paper observed. "[E]very home may now have its distilling plant!"

A few captured stills were admired by both the police and the public. When the law captured what was purported to be "the finest still in the country," it was put on display at the sheriff's office. "It [was] made from a wash-boiler," the *Miner* described, "coppered and rigged-up with a number of attachments necessary under certain circumstances."

One large still "and its supposed product" was put on display in a store window downtown. The *Miner* reported that "suspicions at the authenticity of the product were quieted by a sign which confirmed the common opinion that 'If it comes from Biles-Lockhart's it must be good.'"

One ignorant moonshining practice came to light in September 1920, when law enforcement found a still that was not made of copper but of galvanized iron. This decision to try to utilize a cheaper still could have proven deadly. Distillation produces ethers and acetic acid, which corrode the zinc in the galvanized lining, producing a deadly poison: zinc acetate. The perpetrator, Matt O'Gulin, located his still near the Jerome city dump. He insisted that the brew was for his own personal use. "The county attorney thought it was a case where the arrest of the distiller saved his life," the *Miner* quipped. Within weeks, three more galvanized iron stills were found around Jerome; one was hidden in a combination coop and dog kennel. The irony of the stills' location "in the heart of the world's most solid copper camp" was not lost on the paper.

Claire Champie Cordes also related the story of an unfortunate moonshiner who employed galvanized metal:

> *There was one old fellow, we called him "Lousy Wag," who had set up stills all over the country. The officers couldn't catch him, but they destroyed his stills. For a while, he made good whiskey, but he kept rigging up makeshift stills until it got so rank that one was afraid to drink it. He had one about a mile above our place. Fred said he used an old galvanized wash tub to cook the mask and a wool blanket to catch the alcohol as it went off in steam. When the blanket became saturated, he would squeeze it out into a bucket. He kept a few chickens around to clean up slops of grain. When people found out about Wag's distillery method, they quit buying from* [him], *and he went out of business. The last I heard of old Wag, he was in jail for killing an old man. I think he had lost his mind from drinking the raw whiskey and had beaten an old prospector to death.*

One man was arrested on North Cortez Street when an undersheriff revealed "as shiny a copper still as one could wish to see" in the rear of his car. The man stated that he planned to take it to the state fair in Phoenix; "he must have heard that there were great crowds attending...but could not have heard, as some in Prescott have, that Canadian Club in quart bottles [was] the prevailing tipple there at the time," the *Miner* divulged.

What was described only as a "unique sort of still" was seized and kept "for future reference." Perhaps it was disguised to look like something other than a still.

The king of Yavapai County stills was captured off a "lofty perch on Mingus Mountain," the *Miner* reported. It could cook a whopping seven hundred gallons of mash. George Ruffner led a three-day search for it.

Corn and rye were used by most moonshiners, although one Ash Fork man employed raisins.

By April 1922, the courthouse vault had become crammed with stills and other "booze machinery," so the sheriff's office destroyed it all and sold it for scrap. "All different kinds of stills" were completely wrecked, the *Miner* reported. Even the spiral copper condensing tubes known as worms were cut into lengths so short that "not enough was saved to make a gasoline feed for a motorcycle."

The cat and mouse game of Prohibition would continue in Arizona and the United States until 1931.

20

PRESCOTT RUNS OUT OF WATER

By Drew Desmond

It would be the biggest disaster to befall Prescott since the Great Fire of 1900. By the time the summer of 1919 came along, water pressure had consistently fallen so low that everyone was required to boil it. Unfortunately, that did nothing to relieve the water of its foul smell.

The main reason for the water shortage was escalating population growth. Part of that growth included the renewal of Fort Whipple into a hospital. Yet even before it was in full operation, the hospital was already consuming most of the water that could be pumped from Del Rio Springs, the largest source and producer of fresh water for the city.

The city's fathers had already become aware of the impending shortage the previous year and decided on a stopgap measure. Because of "the difficulty in sinking wells in that part of the county," the *Miner* pointed out, Prescott had been allowing farmers in the Chino Valley and Jerome Junction area to tap into the line for their domestic use for several years. They paid the same rate as the city dwellers. However, in May 1918, the city turned off the tap.

This caused a group of farmers to appear before the chamber of commerce to protest the decision. "The [farmer's] spokesman, Mr. Carbine, told the gathering that the city had taken its action at the very worst time of the year," the *Miner* recorded, "when the farmers were all busy putting out their gardens and crops, and unless the city granted the settlers an extension of time in which to procure another water supply, great hardship will be worked on the tillers of the soil, in that the production of crops in that section [would] be materially curtailed."

Prescott's city clerk Frank Whisman was on hand to explain the city's reasoning. In fact, the city didn't really have the right to sell the water outside its limits, and it could be stopped by a single taxpayer's objection. Additionally, "the continual opening and shutting of taps connected directly with the trunk water mains caused a great deal of damage both to the pipes and to the pumps," the *Miner* declared. Indeed, installing a household tap into the main line is highly impractical. Water would rocket from the faucet with the pressure of a fire hydrant. It would sting, and potentially even injure one's hands under the seven-hundred-pounds-per-square-inch force.

"There was an impending water shortage," Whisman continued, "and since the city had grown so large [with a population of nearly 8,000] and the use of water had increased proportionately that it was a matter of self-protection to cease selling water to the tract settlers." Prescott also learned that "the city would [soon] be held to have furnished this service for such a long time that it would be obliged to continue the arrangement indefinitely" if it continued the practice much longer.

Another move the city made to conserve water occurred in January 1919, when Prescott won a restraining order to stop the Santa Fe Railroad from building a dam across Miller Creek. The city also sued the railroad for the cost of the water it had taken from there.

Even after cutting off the northern rural customers and the railroad, Prescott was still consuming more water than was being captured. In December 1918, over 17 million gallons were consumed. The previous December, that number was only 10 million.

Demand on the city's water infrastructure was at its maximum when disaster struck October 1, 1918. "Caused either by defective wiring or an overheated stove," the *Miner* suggested, fire destroyed the water plant at Del Rio Springs. One of the workers took a short walk, returning to find the roof engulfed in flames. A short hose was used to combat the fire, but it rapidly spread "to the engine room, igniting the oil-soaked interior," and the building burned to the ground. The damage was estimated to cost $75,000, or about twenty-two years' pay for the average worker at the time. In response, a mile of pipeline was built to divert Banning Creek water to the Groom Creek plant "in sufficient quantity not only to supply all possible needs of the enlarged [Whipple] post but possibly to leave a surplus for city use."

Lynx Lake in the 1960s. *Ruffner Archives.*

Initially, plans were discussed to repair the Del Rio plant, but it was realized that harvesting water from that location was both ignorant and tremendously wasteful. It was found that the Del Rio Springs were ultimately fed by the rains and snows of the mountains that surrounded Prescott and then flowed into Granite Creek, which ran right through town. Instead of capturing the water at the source in the nearby mountains, Prescott was waiting for it to flow 20 miles away and descend 1,100 feet before pumping it back to the city. This was costing water customers a whopping sixty cents to produce one thousand gallons of water, making the average monthly water bill over one-quarter of a week's pay. If the water was captured in the mountains above the city and gravity was employed to move it, this cost would shrink to two cents. So, the idea of installing 20 miles of wider pipes and larger pumps at Del Rio was quickly dismissed. Fortunately, some repairs were able to be made, and some water was delivered to the new Fort Whipple Hospital complex, but they were now absorbing every drop of it.

Two possible dam sites were studied as early as the late nineteenth century: Potts (now Butte) Creek and Aspen Creek. When Harry Heap took over as mayor in February 1919, he favored the Potts Creek site. However, neither Del Rio, Potts Creek nor Aspen Creek ended up being used.

Eventually, the damming of Banning Creek would solve the problem. It would take four years to build this new dam and for water to be harvested from it. The new reservoir was named Lake Goldwater, and it could hold one hundred million gallons of fresh water. It was estimated that the city of eight thousand would now have enough water to serve a population of fifty thousand, an incomprehensible number at that time.

Before the project was completed, however, it would take strict conservation and the grace of wet weather to see Prescott through its water crisis.

Due to Depression-era work programs, in the 1930s, the amount of water held in Prescott's reservoir increased greatly with the construction of Upper Goldwater Lake.

21

BARRY GOLDWATER'S ONE REGRET

By Bradley G. Courtney

Whiskey Row of Prescott is arguably the most fascinating quarter–city block in the western United States. The centerpiece of this historic, jam-packed street has been the magnificent Palace Saloon, today the Palace Restaurant and Saloon. It's no wonder that one of Arizona's favorite sons, Barry Goldwater, whose ties to Prescott are well documented, once lamented, "My only regret is that I didn't buy the Palace when I had a chance."

His friend Tom Sullivan, who, in 1977, believed he had purchased the Palace, knew this. So, on July 26 of that year, when writing Goldwater, his incentive was rather thinly veiled and his guilt a bit transparent. The bulk of his letter, however, disclosed his plans to restore the saloon to its early 1900s glory and to share its considerable history with its patrons. "I know of your very deep and sentimental interest in Prescott, and any help that you may be able to give will be greatly appreciated."

Goldwater's response was a truly honest, magnanimous and typically humorous letter, dated August 10, 1977. It began with a good-natured, "You rascal, you went and bought what had long been my desire to own. When I was in China during World War II, I received in a Christmas package a book, and I knew when I opened it, there would be the deed to the Palace Bar, which, at that time, was available." According to Goldwater, the asking price then was a mere $20,000. He went on to share some personal contacts to assist Sullivan in his undertaking, followed by two unforgettable tales involving the Palace. The first is said to have occurred in 1889, and it is regarded the transference of the territorial capital site from Prescott to Phoenix.

Goldwater wrote:

> *As you know, the second floor was a house of prostitution. I think the original brass beds are still up there, as well as the bed pans, cuspidors, etc. There is a story that Bert Fireman can elaborate on for you involving the movement of the capital to Phoenix. The story is that the leader of the senate, having one glass eye, had it stolen during the night. As a result, he couldn't take his place in the territorial senate* [the next day], *and the lack of his vote sent the capital to Phoenix.*

According to the story, which is said to have occurred in the Palace Hotel above the saloon, this vainglorious scoundrel who represented Yavapai County and, therefore, Prescott had a favorite "lady of the night"—"Kissin' Jenny"—working at the Palace. She, so the legend says, was thus hired by some Phoenician politicians to steal the politician's fake eye. They predicted that this delegate's vanity would prevent him from attending the voting session that was scheduled for the next day, even with the issue of the territorial capital at stake.

Did anything like this happen? Unfortunately, historians often find themselves popping fiction bubbles, and this is one of those times.

For starters, the Palace Hotel did not exist until 1901.

"Kissin' Jenny" is a great story, and something like it might have happened in Prescott; there is even evidence suggesting that Mary Thorne, the wife of D.C. Thorne, who was the proprietor of the Palace at that time, operated a prostitution house on Montezuma Street.

Even if Kissin' Jenny worked there, however, she is not to blame for the capital being relocated to Phoenix rather than remaining in Prescott. Some stubborn facts get in the way. Legislative Act No. 1 was signed by Governor Conrad Zulick on January 26, 1889, moving the capital to Phoenix. The vote passed by seven votes and "was railroaded through both houses at the rate of sixty miles an hour." The only councilman absent was a representative from Apache County. He was home attending to a sick child. All Yavapai County legislators were present for the vote.

The second anecdote from "Mr. Conservative" was equally amusing and survives as a testament to the celebrated wit of the five-term senator.

It involved Barney Smith, a co-owner of the Palace beginning in 1901 who became its sole owner in 1909. Goldwater wrote:

> *I always can remember old man Smith would go to work at eight in the morning, walk behind the bar, grab any bottle at hand and start the day's drinking. Around four, his wife, a very large woman who taught piano, would come in and play and drink beer. The two them would wobble out and go home about six. I am told all he ever ate was raw hamburger, and he lived to be one heck of an old age, so I am taking up raw hamburger with my bourbon.*

Smith still holds the record for the longest stint as a saloon owner on Whiskey Row. His career as a Whiskey Row proprietor started in 1878 with the Plaza Bit Saloon on Montezuma Street. He acquired a 50 percent interest in the Cabinet Saloon in the 1890s, co-owned the Palace Saloon starting in 1901 and became its sole proprietor in 1909, remaining so until 1943.

Tom Sullivan never took ownership of the Palace; the deal fell through in escrow. Nineteen years later, however, Sullivan's idea of capitalizing on the Palace's history came to fruition when Dave "Cowboy Dave" Michelson of California bought the saloon in 1996. He went on to create a museum-like atmosphere therein that has attracted people from all over the world. It still does.

22

"THE BOSS" TAKES OVER WHISKEY ROW

By Bradley G. Courtney

It was September 1989, and Bruce Springsteen wanted to see the Grand Canyon. "The Boss" mounted his silver and blue Harley-Davidson and rode out of Los Angeles along with four of his friends/bodyguards. Three rode alongside Springsteen while the fourth followed in a van. Springsteen's desire to see one of the seven natural wonders of the world would lead to an impromptu—and if you ask bartender Brenda "Bubbles" Pechanec (who later reverted to her given name, Brenda Phillips) and others who were there—magical experience on the afternoon of Friday, September 29, in Prescott at Matt's Saloon. And for Bubbles, it would be life changing.

Matt's, a popular honky-tonk bar that is still thriving on Whiskey Row that featured such artists as Waylon Jennings and Buck Owens on its balconied stage back in the 1960s, suddenly became the equivalent to Madison Square Garden that fall day. Therein occurred an hour-long episode that became national news, the stuff of legend and a story that is still oft told today.

The weather was typical Prescott perfect. The cool of the morning had given way to low humidity, comfortable warmth in the afternoon. Sometime before 2:00 p.m., Springsteen rode into town, entered the Palace and, according to a girl who was so excited, she could barely remember her name when asked, enjoyed a couple of Coca-Colas. Perhaps because no live music was playing at the Palace that day, Springsteen and his posse decided to head over to Matt's Saloon, where the Mile High Band—the saloon's house band—was playing.

When they walked into the near-empty bar at about 2 that afternoon, thirty-nine-year-old Bubbles Pechanec could not have known that she was about to be a part of one of rock-and-roll history's most beloved tales. Bubbles, who had just remarried for the eighth time on July 4 of that year (yes, Mr. Pechanec was husband number eight), had been enjoying the calm that came with a Friday afternoon on the Row, but on this day, it was a short-lived calm. The calm indeed came before the proverbial storm. The underwhelming day was about to become overwhelming.

Some biker friends of Bubbles—she was a biker girl herself—had told her that some biker-looking dudes were heading her way. One friend told her that one of them had asked where they could find "biker chicks." Perhaps, however, her friends were preparing her, knowing that she had, just that week, returned to work after months of chemotherapy and radiation to combat stomach and vaginal cancer.

Springsteen and his posse sat down at the bar and ordered drinks. One was wearing sunglasses and peering over the top of them, as if to hide his identity. This did not fool Bubbles. "I know who you are. Don't try to hide from me!" she told the world's biggest rock star. And from then on, he did not hide. There he was. The Boss. Tanned, relaxed and, according to Bubbles and others present that day, down to earth.

That is when the fun began. Bottles of Budweiser were bought. Small talk was had. It seemed to Bubbles that Springsteen was just enjoying being one of the boys. Somehow, the conversation came around to how many times Bubbles had been married, which the Boss found amusing. Bubbles took no offense. This went on for about fifteen minutes. What she did not talk about were her medical issues and mounting hospital bills, even though they were a concern, as she had not been working during her treatment and even now was receiving a mere $1.25 an hour plus tips.

Soon, the boys of the Mile High Band realized who was in their midst. Danny Orr, the rhythm guitarist and harmonica player, climbed down from Matt's stage to tell his drummer, Jimmy Morehaus, that the Boss was sitting at the bar. The drummer thought he meant Matt Butitta, the owner of the saloon. When he was told that Danny was referring to Bruce Springsteen, Morehaus rolled his eyes and responded, "Yeah, right."

Then he realized it was no joke. Why not take advantage of it? Morehaus had written a song, "I Don't Mind." Would the Boss listen to it? Of course, he would. And he did. And not only that—he said he liked it.

Stories vary as to how Springsteen wound up on stage. One is that a member of the band did not believe the guy they were talking to was really the Boss—that he was a faker—and because of that, Springsteen wanted to prove he was the one and only. What is known is that after some conversation, Bruce jumped up from the bar and shouted to the Prescott musicians, "C'mon boys, let's jam!" Suddenly, to the astonishment of the gathering crowd, there was a world-famous rock star climbing up the stairs, appearing on the stage where they had seen so many local acts, and being handed Orr's Stratocaster guitar. Mile High Band member Dave Kellerman arrived late and climbed up to the stage, where the newest band member stuck out his hand and introduced himself: "Hey man, I'm Bruce."

Sometime after that, according to Bubbles, Kellerman had a conversation with the Boss about the bartender's medical issues and hospital bills. That conversation may have occurred in the saloon bathroom. As Kellerman and Springsteen walked into the bathroom, one of the rock star's bodyguards followed. Looking back, Springsteen told the man, "We'll take it from here."

Word got around town that something of a surreal nature was happening in Matt's Saloon. A co-owner of Hotel St. Michael's got on the payphone in front of Matt's and started making phone calls. One observer, Steve Brennan, noted, "The whole thing just didn't seem like it was really happening." Brennan, a local journalist and newspaper editor almost apologetically admitted to his readers that "I could barely stop staring at Springsteen long enough to ask him to allow a photograph, much less an interview." Bubbles was no longer serving liquor, because suddenly, no one was interested in drinking.

Touring-wise, 1989 was a down year for Springsteen. He was pining to jam. For almost an hour, the Boss performed with the Mile High Band to a frenzied audience. Chuck Berry's "Sweet Sixteen" and Elvis Presley's "Don't Be Cruel" were covered. Springsteen's version of "Route 66" was a particular crowd-pleaser. Danny Orr said that he has seen enthusiasm from a crowd as a member of the Mile High Band, but this was at a level where he himself felt what it was like to be a rock star.

The only Springsteen original played that afternoon was his sultry 1985 hit "I'm on Fire." It is with this song that came one of the most heartwarming parts of this epic story. While Springsteen was performing, one of his companions called out to Bubbles. The Boss was clearly focused on making Bubbles's day; he wanted to know what her favorite song was, the bodyguard said. "I'm on Fire," she answered without hesitation and without realizing he wasn't necessarily asking what her favorite Springsteen song was. Minutes later, she was being serenaded by the superstar, right there in Matt's Saloon, as she listened from behind the bar.

After that, the band requested another original, his "Pink Cadillac." To the band's amusement, Bruce told them he could not remember all the words. Some later concluded it must have been because he was too drunk to do so. The truth, however, is that "Pink Cadillac" was the non-album B-side to his 1984 single "Dancing in the Dark" and not one he often played. In fact, it was made famous not by the Boss but as a hit single by pop diva Natalie Cole the year before.

When he finished the set, he came down off the stage to a hyper-excited atmosphere. Images show him smiling and walking with a Budweiser in each hand. Matt's was getting more crowded by the second, so Springsteen jumped over the bar, grabbed Bubbles and gave her a kiss. Probably knowing his time was growing short—as far as keeping the situation manageable—he refused to be interviewed but allowed the local press to take some photographs as he hammed it up with Bubbles, telling the crowd he had come to Prescott to become her husband number nine.

The scene was still under control but was growing more chaotic as word continued to rapidly spread that Bruce Springsteen was in Matt's Saloon. While he was having a good time up on the stage, the people in Matt's numbered about ninety. Now the crowd on Whiskey Row was growing, spilling out onto Montezuma Street and even the Courthouse Plaza. Orr labeled it "mad city." Similarly, Bubbles said it was becoming "mug city" for the icon. "People were grabbing for him like they wanted to tear his clothes off. It was almost like a riot was about to start," she said. "Before they all knew who he was, he was having a good time—talking to the regulars and drinking beer."

Indeed, businessowners along the Row were closing their shops and racing toward Matt's as news of Bruce's presence continued to spread like wildfire. With little security and the situation frenzying, it was time to for the Boss to make his escape. And so, he did. His bodyguards carved a path through the crowd, and then Springsteen and his boys mounted their cycles and headed down Whiskey Row and out of town.

By the look on his face in photographs, the Boss clearly enjoyed the experience as much as anyone else. Danny Orr exclaimed, "He was one of the nicest guys I ever met. [Springsteen] had no airs, and when he gets on the stage, he's in total control."

That night, the Mile High Band resumed playing to a larger, more excited crowd than usual. The people probably had in the back of their minds that the Boss might return. He did come back to Prescott but not to Matt's. What Prescottonians did not know at the time—and most still do not realize—is that Springsteen and his comrades had reservations at Hotel St. Michael for that evening. According to one old-timer who had been doing some construction work in the hotel fifty yards up Montezuma Street from Matt's, Springsteen and his crew, under the cover of darkness, used the fire escape on the backside of St. Michael to enter the building. They rode off quietly the next morning to see the Grand Canyon.

Danny Orr said it best, "Nowhere in my wildest dreams did I think I'd jam with the Boss!"

This story became even more legendary a few days later. At the time of this writing, Bubbles—who now goes by Bubbles Phillips—is seventy-one years old and suffering from the effects of three heart attacks and two strokes, but she can tell her story lucidly with engaging animation and a twinkle in her eye.

Some narratives wrongly claim that Springsteen left a big tip for Bubbles that very day. Others assert that a check was sent in the mail directly to Bubbles. She straightens that all out: "I got a call."

"I don't remember exactly," she said. "It was two or three days later. I know everybody says I got a check. I never got a check. I got a call."

A local newspaper reporter heard the news before she did and gave her a ring. She told her that her hospital bills had been paid in full. Bubbles's personal check to the hospital had been returned earlier, which had been a mystery to her. Upon hearing this staggering news, she was shocked.

There was more. Bubbles asked, "Who did this?" But the reporter did not know. So, the bartender called the Yavapai Regional Medical Center. Sure enough, she learned that the entire $160,000 she owed was no longer a concern. It had indeed been paid.

"By whom?" Bubbles asked.

"Bruce Springsteen," came the answer.

To this day, Bubbles says she is stunned and does not have the words to express her gratitude. "God bless the Boss," she said.

Bubbles was divorced from Mr. Pechanec a month after meeting Springsteen. She never found husband number nine.

Brenda "Bubbles" Phillips passed away in 2022 while this book was being written, as did her dear friend Dave Kellerman, who shared the stage with the Boss that day. Both will be fondly remembered on Whiskey Row.

BIBLIOGRAPHY

Books

Banks, Leo. *Rattlesnake Blues: Dispatches from a Snakebit Territory*. Phoenix: Arizona Highways Books, 2000.

Cordes, Claire Champie. *Ranch Trails and Short Tales.* Prescott, AZ: Crown King Press, 1991.

Courtney, Bradley G. *Prescott's Original Whiskey Row*. Charleston, SC: The History Press, 2015.

———. *The Whiskey Row Fire of 1900*. Charleston, SC: The History Press, 2020.

Prescott, William H. *The History of the Conquest of Mexico*. New York: Harper and Brothers, 1843.

Walker, Dale L. *Rough Rider: Buckey O'Neill of Arizona*. Lincoln: University of Nebraska Press, 1975.

Wells, Edmund. *Argonaut Tales: Stories of the Gold Seekers and the Indian Scouts of Early Arizona.* Illustrated by Evan T. Wilson. New York: Frederick H. Hitchcock, 1927.

Journals

Bates, Al. "Arizona Escapes from New Mexico." *Territorial Times* 7, no. 2 (May 2014).

———. "Gold Is Discovered in the Central Arizona Highlands." *Territorial Times* 7, no. 2 (May 2014).

———. "Prescott Celebrates the Fourth of July." *Territorial Times* 7, no. 2 (May 2014).

Collins, Thomas P. "Dan Thorne: A Whiskey Row Success Story." *Territorial Times* 4, no. 2 (May 2011).

Goldberg, Isaac. "An Old Timer's Experience in Arizona." *Arizona Historical Review* 2, no. 3 (October 1929).

Articles

Arp, Jennifer. "Preserving History: Restored Masonic Temple Monument to Proud Past." Prescott Public Library vertical file.

Collins, Thomas P. "Andrew L. Moeller: Pioneer, Entrepreneur, Philanthropist." Parts 1 and 2. Sharlot Hall Museum "Days Past" Archives. May 20 and May 27, 2010.

Courtney, Bradley G. "Barry Goldwater's One Regret: 'You Rascal You…'." Sharlot Hall Museum "Days Past" Archives. September 12, 2012.

———. "Betting on the Baby on the Bar." *True West Magazine*, December 2018.

———. "Famous Highwayman 'Brazen Bill' Brazelton Meets Whiskey Row's D.C. Thorne." Sharlot Hall Museum "Days Past" Archives. February 4, 2017.

———. "The Juniper House: Prescott's First Restaurant." Sharlot Hall Museum "Days Past" Archives. December 7, 2019.

———. "The Legend of the Quartz Rock Saloon and the Origins of Whiskey Row." Sharlot Hall Museum "Days Past" Archives. March 1, 2014.

———. "Prescott's Most Famous Saloon Story: Legend vs. Truth." Parts 1 and 2. Sharlot Hall Museum "Days Past" Archives. May 3 and 10, 2014.

———. "Whiskey Row's Buckey O'Neill." Parts 1 and 2. Sharlot Hall Museum "Days Past" Archives. March 17 and 25, 2018.

———. "Whiskey Row's Dynamic 'D.C.' Thorne." Parts 1 and 2. Sharlot Hall Museum "Days Past" Archives. November 18 and 25, 2017.

Goldwater, Morris. "The History of Aztlan Lodge." Prescott Public Library vertical file.

Gorby, Richard. "Prescott's First 4th of July: No Fireworks or Women." Sharlot Hall Museum "Days Past" Archives. June 28, 1997.

Kimball, Richard. "Days Past: Ol' Mike Served as a Guardian of the Plaza." *Prescott Courier*, April 21, 1996.

Lowe, Sam. "In Memory of Mike at Prescott's Courthouse Plaza." Arizona Oddities. 2014. www.arizonaoddities.com.

Markum, J. "Early Day Bigwigs Were Masons." Prescott Public Library vertical file.

Woodbury, Chuck. "Mike the Dog Remembered." RVTravel. 2017. www.rvtravel.com.

Interviews

Interview/tour with Greg W. "Scotty" Hays, educational technologist, Aztlan Lodge no. 1. 2018.

Collections

Disasters: Walnut Grove Dam. Vertical file. Sharlot Hall Museum Library and Archives.

Newspapers

Arizona Gazette
Arizona Journal-Miner
Arizona Miner
Arizona Republican
Arizona Weekly Journal-Miner
Arizona Weekly Miner
Courier (Prescott)
Phoenix Herald
Prescott Courier
Prescott Courier Territorial Days Extra
Prescott Evening Courier
Prescott Journal-Miner
Prescott Weekly Courier
Tombstone Epitaph
Weekly Arizona Journal-Miner
Weekly Arizona Miner
Weekly Journal-Miner

ABOUT THE AUTHORS

Bradley G. Courtney, the author of *Prescott's Original Whiskey Row* and *The Whiskey Row Fire of 1900* and coauthor with Drew Desmond of *Murder and Mayhem in Prescott*, is an independent historian who lived and taught in Phoenix, Arizona, for nineteen years and on the Navajo Indian Reservation in northern Arizona for twelve years. During six of his years on the reservation, he was also a riverboat pilot and guide who gave tours down the incomparable canyons of the Colorado River. Brad has also recorded four albums of original music and has appeared on CNN, the Travel Channel and numerous other television stations across the country. He holds a master's degree in history from California State University.

Along with *Murder and Mayhem in Prescott*, Drew Desmond is the author of the immensely popular *#PrescottAZHistory* blog, which features almost three hundred articles and has welcomed nearly 750,000 readers. Local schools use Drew's blog in their classroom curriculum, and his research finds are displayed in two museums. He has also authored many magazine articles. His social media pages are followed by newspapers,

television stations, businesses, politicians and even towns. He is the secretary of the Board of the Prescott Western Heritage Foundation and its Western Heritage Center on historic Whiskey Row. He spends time at the center weekly as its mercantile manager and docent. Come and say hello!